THE GIFT OF PAIN

THE GIFT OF PAIN

AN INVITATION TO SHIFT YOUR PERSPECTIVE, RECLAIM YOUR POWER, AND TRANSFORM YOUR LIFE

HELEN MACMILLAN

Hardcover ISBN: 978-1-955811-23-1

Paperback ISBN: 978-1-955811-24-8

E-book ISBN: 978-1-955811-26-2

LCCN: 2022908138

First hardcover edition: July 2022

Edited by WorldChangers Media / www.WorldChangers.media

Cover photo by Kirth Bobb / www.kirthbobb.com

Cover design by Michael Rehder / www.rehderandcompanie.com

Design & Typesetting by Paul Baillie-Lane / www.pblpublishing.com

Published by WorldChangers Media

PO Box 83, Foster, RI 02825

www.WorldChangers.Media

DEDICATION

This book is dedicated to all those doing the inner work of self-discovery. To the seekers, who never stop growing and evolving, who refuse to settle or accept that this is all there is or that they have to learn to live with their pain, who never give up hope that there is something better.

To those who are committed to living their most fulfilling, joyful, and abundant life—thank you for being on this journey with me.

PRAISE

"On the other side of your pain is the next level of your power. This book is a guide to upleveling your leadership."

- Rich Litvin, Founder of 4PC and coauthor of *The Prosperous Coach*

"It's challenging to focus on achieving your dreams when you're in any type of pain. Helen's book is an essential read for anyone who is looking to shed their limiting habits, stop their self-sabotage, and provides a pathway for freeing you to experience more joy and fulfillment."

- Maya Marcia Wieder, CEO of Dream University and bestselling author

"Helen is a gifted teacher and coach who has transformed her own life and now empowers others to do the same. In this book she shares a simple, yet powerful 5-step process you can use again and again to make profound shifts in your own life by letting pain be your greatest teacher and guide."

- Jack Canfield, coauthor of the *Chicken Soup for the Soul®* series and *The Success Principles™*

"In her new book, *The Gift of Pain*, author Helen MacMillan shares a potent personal journey of discovering how embracing the unthinkable becomes a gift. She details a natural way your pain can become a roadmap to health."

- Deborah Sandella PhD, RN, international bestselling author of *Goodbye Hurt & Pain*

"The most important thing to me in deciding whom I learn from is knowing that the teacher has integrated what they are teaching. Helen MacMillan practices in her own life everything she teaches in *The Gift of Pain*. This work is being birthed from an embodied place. Helen holds nothing back in her sharing, helping to inspire the reader to look within and heal their own heart."

- Darla LeDoux, Author of *Shift the Field* and CEO of Sourced

"If you are a human being, you have experienced pain in one form or another. Pain is a revelatory teacher, and had I known its true wisdom, I might not have resisted it for as long as I did. It took me until my mid-forties to understand it as an invitation to reveal, feel, and heal my way back home to myself, and while it's never comfortable, I now understand it to be the true guide that it is. Helen has graced us with a beautiful testament to pain and its many gifts in her beautiful book. Not only will you appreciate her insight, but you will welcome her as a seasoned guide to help you through the hardest parts."

- Monica Rodgers, Founder of The Revelation Project and The Revelation Project Podcast

"What an extraordinary gift Helen MacMillan has given us with *The Gift of Pain.* In language that is as sparkling and clear as life-giving water, this relatable work doesn't shy away from Helen's own passage through pain. Instead, she reveals the dark country of her own grief, depression, and self-doubt before showing us, stumbling step-by-step, her own path to awareness and healing. In a voice that is compassionate, loving, trustworthy, and wise, Helen encourages us to embrace our own journey through difficult emotions, recognizing them as messengers that can point the way toward growth and restoration. Without judgment, and with complete faith in our ability to love ourselves back to wholeness, Helen guides us in how we can heed the lessons of our physical and spiritual bodies to create expansion, lightness, and peace. A beautiful and necessary book!"

- Rosemarie Robotham, Writer, Editor, Literary collaborator at RosemarieRobotham.com

CONTENTS

PART III:

RECEIVING THE GIFTS OF PAIN

PREFACE

There is the pain of unfulfilled potential
and dreams unrealized.

The pain caused by deep disappointments.

The pain of loss.

The pain of core wounds around being "enough," "worthy," and "lovable."

We unconsciously create sophisticated defense mechanisms to protect ourselves from feeling pain. They help us to cope–to survive.

And, like many of the pharmaceutical drugs that help us to survive potentially life-threatening illnesses, they can have serious side effects.

The consequences of shutting down your wounded heart, dampening your feelings, and cutting yourself off from your "inner GPS" can be devastating.

Disconnecting from your heart has far-reaching consequences on your ability to connect with your deepest desires and know your own truth.

Your feelings are meant to give you the information to guide you through life. When you ignore them, you end up feeling lost and alone, disconnected from your joy, depressed. Life is not as vibrant or colorful. Your energy becomes dull and, over time, your health declines, too.

Without the connection to your heart—the seat of love—you are more likely to be driven by fear. You are less confident. You are locked into survival mode, where it is impossible to truly thrive.

If you are here, reading this, it's because a part of you knows there is more to life than what you are currently experiencing. You are already beginning to awaken.

Here's what I want you to know before we go any further:

Your pain is here to serve you. To bring something to your awareness so you can make changes that will improve your life in some way. Pain *always* has a purpose. Once you understand that, and receive its message—its *gift*—the pain is no longer necessary and it disappears.

You are not broken, and you do not need to be fixed. You may feel like you are, but if you keep coming from this premise, you're trying to solve the wrong problem and you won't find what you are looking for.

I invite you to embrace any painful or challenging experience by viewing it from this perspective. Breathe into it. Stop beating up on yourself, blaming, shaming, or judging yourself for where you are. This only serves to keep you stuck.

With pain as your guide, you are about to embark on a journey of awakening to the truth of who you *already* are.

INTRODUCTION

Life is magical and beautiful.
And when we are in pain, it does
not feel that way.

Pain can feel unbearable, overwhelming, uncontrollable, and maddening. It pushes us out of our zone of comfort and safety, leaving us feeling alone and afraid.

It's no wonder we instinctively resist pain. We say things like, "I don't have time for this!" or "This couldn't have happened at a worse time!"

If we have no control over our situation, we may feel like a victim of circumstance, wondering, *What have I done to deserve this?* or *Why me?*

Here's what I know for sure: how we perceive, judge, interpret, or analyze a situation dictates how we react. And this perception can actually determine whether or not we find something to be painful.

When we perceive something as "bad" or "wrong," we react very differently than if we perceive it as "right" or "good." We tend to resist the "bad/wrong" and embrace the "good/right."

One perspective elicits feelings of heaviness, doubt, shame, anxiety ... fear. The other evokes feelings of lightness, happiness, openness, and excitement ... love.

But what if we perceived the painful experiences of our lives differently?

What if these challenges were giving us an opportunity to change something for the better? To heal—become more whole and powerful—and experience something new that enables us to grow and expand?

What if these experiences were designed to give us the opportunity to practice responding differently and applying the wisdom we've gained from past experiences?

What if we automatically assumed that our pain has a *positive* purpose? That it has a really important message for us? That its intention is to powerfully serve, support, and guide us to live in alignment with our greatest joy, desires, purpose, and potential?

I truly believe it does.

And when you choose this perspective, each painful or challenging experience becomes an opportunity for new insights. You will be surprised and delighted, again and again—as I have been—by the magnificent perfection of life. Your life becomes more of a joyful adventure, with you in the role of the powerful creator rather than a woeful victim.

My intention in writing this book is to share some of the insights I've gained from my own life experiences, along with more than thirty-eight years of working with the body, mind, and soul—as a physical therapist, healer, teacher, and transformational life coach, helping my clients find relief for their physical and emotional pain, often where nothing else has helped.

I've learned that when we acknowledge our pain, shift our perspective on it, and open to receive and respond to the messages it brings, it can lead to incredible transformation and healing.

It is my heartfelt desire that this book will help you change any perception you have of pain as the "enemy," or as an indicator that you did something "wrong" or didn't do something "right."

The information and stories I share are intended to help you understand the value of embracing your pain—as a messenger, a friend, a gift—so that you can utilize it as a doorway to finding deeper levels of self-love, truth, joy, peace, and freedom. The practical tools and processes will help you do the work. This is where the shift happens that opens the door to magic and miracles!

Finally, my deepest wish is that what you read here will inspire you to open your heart to yourself and trust it to guide you on your own unique journey to ever-expanding levels of joy, fulfillment, abundance, and purpose.

PART I

UNDERSTANDING PAIN

CHAPTER 1

CRACKED OPEN

I reach for the bottle of Valium in the medicine cabinet and pour the contents onto the counter. I want to go to sleep and not wake up.

Tears streaming down my face, I begin to swallow them two and three at a time until I finish the entire bottle. My heart literally hurts. I just want the pain to stop.

The voices in my head are deafening.

The woman at the burial: *What a shame the prettier of the two of you died.*

The server at the patty shop: *How can you be smiling when your sister just died two weeks ago?*

My dad: *What's wrong with you? Why are you out on the street every night?*

My boyfriend: *Helen, I think we should take a break right now.*

Feelings of shame, abandonment, heartache, and judgment sit on my chest like a heavy weight.

My chest feels squeezed. It's hard to breathe.

I don't remember exactly what brought it all to a head that day, and writing this now, I feel ashamed about that—about not being clear, not remembering the exact details of the moment I decided to end my one precious life.

I know I had an argument with Dad about something that day.

I know I left his office feeling like shit.

I know I ended up at my house. But I don't know how I got there.

I know my best friend, Dotty, was with me.

But the details are sparse, sketchy, faded.

Elizabeth and I were only fourteen months apart. Our parents used to dress us like twins. Same stylish dress—hers green, mine yellow—and the same hairstyle—parted in two, with long drop curls and ribbons that matched our dresses. We were inseparable as children and shared a bedroom, often talking and giggling after lights out.

I was away at college in 1981 when I got the call that Elizabeth was in a bad car accident on the way to the beach with friends.

The heartbreak that came with her death exacerbated the emotional pain I was already carrying due to many emotional wounds that were never fully addressed, including my parents' separation. On top of that, I grew up as an empath, with the ability to feel other people's emotions deeply, and yet I had no idea what this was, or what to do with it. I could clearly see and feel a dissonance between what the adults around me were feeling and what they were actually expressing. I didn't understand why, and I often felt confused, angry, misunderstood, and, quite frankly, crazy.

My parents knew how to treat a broken arm or a bleeding cut, especially with my mother being a nurse, but they were wholly unprepared for dealing with emotional wounds—both theirs and mine. There was no compassionate acknowledgment of what I was expressing. My emotional outbursts were either ignored or punished, so I trained myself to repress them. I locked my feelings away with the other "unacceptable" and misunderstood parts of myself.

Suicidal thoughts were not new to me, but in the month following Elizabeth's funeral, I was really floundering. Mom was in New York City with her best friend, taking a much-needed break. I felt lost and alone, and the bottle of Valium the doctor had given Mom to cope with the loss became my opportunity.

After downing the contents of the bottle, I called my boyfriend Roger to say "goodbye." Alarmed by my slurred speech, he peppered me with questions and demanded to speak to Dotty. I eventually admitted to taking the pills and Dotty called my older brother, Douglas, who in turn called a friend of my mother's–the head nurse at a local hospital.

Before I knew it, I was being rushed to the emergency room where the hospital staff pumped my stomach and saved my life.

I awoke the next morning in the hospital. Realizing I was still alive, I angrily pulled the IV drip out of my arm.

I pretended to be asleep when the nurse came to check on me, and she gently reinserted the IV, thinking it had fallen out on its own.

As soon as she left, I pulled it out again.

By the time the nurse returned a while later the bed was a bloody, wet mess, and boy was she pissed.

"What's wrong with you, child?!" she shouted angrily. "Don't you know we're trying to help you?"

"I don't want your help! I don't want to be here! Just let me die!" I screamed, tears of frustration rolling down my cheeks.

It was a truly horrible day, one that's painful to recall even after all this time, but there was a glimmer of light in an otherwise dark situation: hospital policy required me to see a psychiatrist in order to be discharged, so I got to talk about my feelings. For the first time, I felt that my pain was truly validated when the psychiatrist explained to my mother: "This was not a cry for attention. Helen really wanted to die."

The pain of my attempted suicide awakened something in my mother and inspired her to say something so powerful that it, in turn, awakened something in me.

She said, "Helen, would you take my most expensive, most favorite, silk dress and cut it into shreds?"

I was shocked and appalled. "Of course not!" I responded.

She replied softly, tears in her eyes, "Well, how could you try to kill yourself? *Don't you think you are worth more to me than a dress?*"

My heart cracked open, and I began to weep. I felt my mother's love for me. I *finally* felt like I mattered. You see, my pain was that of a child screaming to be seen, heard, and acknowledged—to believe that I was important.

I didn't recognize it then, but I had internalized earlier life experiences—my parents' divorce, Dad leaving home, Mom's resulting emotional disconnection. I thought they meant that I was not valuable and that I did not matter.

I desperately needed to hear those words from my mother. It was such a gift.

Maybe you aren't where I was, but if you've ever thought that the only way to escape your pain was to leave it behind, you're not alone. In fact, most of us have been there in some way, shape, or form.

Over the course of more than thirty-eight years as a physical therapist, energy healer, and life coach, I've helped countless people process and find relief from various forms of pain.

It's completely natural to want to avoid pain, or to get rid of it as quickly as possible. Because it feels "bad," we instinctively resist it. We hear too many stories of people who ignored painful indigestion only to die of a heart attack hours later, or who disregarded a nagging pain that turned out to be a deadly cancer that had been festering for a while.

I witnessed this in my own family many years ago. My Aunt Ethlyn, a beautiful, strong, highly educated woman, ignored the lump in her breast until it began to erode through the skin. Her intense fear of a cancer diagnosis stopped her from going to the doctor. We will never know whether she might be alive today if she had gotten treatment sooner.

All too often, we ignore or override our pain, reaching for numbing agents like painkillers and alcohol, or distractions like shopping and overworking, because that's how we learned to deal with it. No one ever taught us how to connect with ourselves and explore the message that our body is sending—or explained that we can even do that!

Ignoring the pain is certainly the easier, more convenient way, and with severe, debilitating pain, it can be hard to even think straight, much less dive in and explore the root cause of it. However, this is just a short-term solution; a Band-Aid, if you will.

What I've learned is this: all pain is a result of how something is perceived and interpreted by the brain.

To understand this better, it's worth taking a look at the different types of pain, the most obvious of which is physical pain. Physical pain begins as a nociceptive impulse sent to the brain from specifi c receptors throughout the body. It is only felt as a physical pain when the brain interprets it as such.

Meanwhile, emotional pain occurs when the mind interprets an experience or interaction as negative, bad, or wrong—based on past experiences, learned beliefs, and the perspectives they create about ourselves, others, and life.

Spiritual pain occurs when there is a level of disconnection between the spirit (or soul) and the physical body. This is usually as a result of some form of trauma.

In my experience, conflict between the ego mind (head) and the spiritual mind (heart) is always present when there is emotional and spiritual pain.

When I practiced physical therapy, I helped my patients get relief from the physical and emotional pain resulting from physical injury or disease. As a life coach and energy healer, I help my clients to process and heal emotional, spiritual, and physical pain by changing the beliefs and behaviors that create them.

As I said previously, all pain is a result of how something is perceived and interpreted by the brain. But there are many things that impact how it is interpreted. Unprocessed emotions held within the body are often at the root of physical pain. Mental thought patterns can contribute to tension held within the muscles and connective tissues of the body.

How we process, perceive, and interpret the information informs our response and can exacerbate and perpetuate the pain. These types of pain do not live in a vacuum. Untreated psychological pain can lead to physical pain and vice versa. Unprocessed emotions held within the body and mind are often at the root of physical pain and disease.

Here is the truth: The pain itself is not the problem. It is a *symptom* of the problem. It is information, a message, a warning. It is designed to get our attention.

The problem is that we have learned to fear pain and judge it as "bad," and what we fear we tend to reject, avoid, and resist. And when we do, it can't help us.

We aren't taught how to be with, relate to, deal with, or handle our pain, so we find ways to cope with it. In the words of Carl Jung, "What we resist persists"—so oftentimes we get locked into the cycle of battling pain instead of healing it.

And what happens is it keeps coming back—and will get increasingly more painful—until we get the message.

There are serious consequences when we have this

kind of relationship with pain—when we don't powerfully engage with it and allow it to serve us.

This is what this book—and our work together—is all about.

CHAPTER 2

HEALING HANDS

The elevator doors open and my breath catches as I instantly recognize the beautiful woman sitting at the entrance to my office floor.

It's Serena. Robert's wife.

My heart is pounding but I nervously smile and politely nod hello as I walk past her. Her warm hello tells me she has no clue who I am.

I know she is here to see me. I continue up the hall to my office, my mind racing, trying to figure out what to do. I want to avoid a shameful confrontation in my office or in front of a client.

I check my appointment book. I have room in my schedule for a couple of hours. I take a deep breath and head down to confront her.

"Hi, I'm Helen," I say, looking her in the eye and extending my hand with what I hope is a confident air. I'm terrified.

"I presume you are here to see me? Want to grab a cup of coffee?"

Here I was at the age of twenty-six: a recently-separated mother of two and proud owner of a growing business, Healing Hands, a massage and physical therapy practice. In the local physical therapy community, I became known as the physical therapist who did "massage," often said in a tone dripping with condescension. Even more unconventional was that my office was located in a popular local hotel.

The beauty of being in a small community is that word of mouth is your best form of advertising. When my massage clients found out I was also a licensed physical therapist, they began asking their medical doctors to write them referrals for me for their physical therapy. Over time, other doctors got to know about me and began referring their patients to me. My business was growing rapidly.

My personal life, on the other hand, was a hot mess. My first husband and I had separated a few months before I started the business, when our boys were only six months and two and a half years old.

The depth of the emotional pain I felt with the ending of my marriage was mostly suppressed as I lost myself in my work. I justified it by telling myself that I didn't have time to fall apart. I had two babies to take care of!

My career success served to boost my self-esteem

and confidence. I had neither the time, nor the inclination, to deal with my grief over my failed marriage or to acknowledge the stress of being a single parent. And the truth is, I still had no clue how to address my emotional challenges.

As a result, the patterns of chaos, confusion, and self-abusive behaviors kept playing out. I smoked heavily, worked hard, and partied equally as hard—burning the candle at both ends.

My internal self-talk was toxic, and the suicidal thoughts were still there. After my experience in the hospital, I knew I would never actually attempt it again. But the feelings didn't magically vanish, either. In one of my darkest moments, fueled by severe depression and anxiety, I briefly contemplated killing my children and then myself. The feeling passed just as quickly as it surfaced, thankfully.

It's important that we start speaking about these things. It seems shameful because we've been taught that to even think such things is shameful, much less to speak about them. Shame wants us to hide, to pretend, and not admit that we are hurting. But the healing only begins when we acknowledge our pain, speak our truth, and allow the light to come in and dispel the darkness.

In an effort to soothe the waves of emotional pain and depression, I turned to religion, which was far less destructive than finding relief in drugs. My friend, Nicole, invited me to a prayer group one evening and I was instantly drawn to the pastor's warm smile and his relaxed, joyful demeanor. This non-denominational community seemed more open-minded and less judgmental than the Anglican church I was raised in.

I started attending church regularly. Midweek Bible study and Friday night prayer vigils became the norm. I boldly challenged this "God" to prove to me that "He" existed. I wanted a personal, tangible experience for myself. I didn't want to rely on other people's testimonies and experiences.

I began experiencing miracles and synchronicities, like the time a complete stranger turned up at my office out of the blue and said God had sent her to pray for me; or when a fellow church member turned up at my home and told me the Holy Spirit told him to bring me a message. On both occasions, I was severely depressed and their messages spoke directly to what I was struggling with at the time.

The love and support I found in the church was a healing balm that saved my life. It served me for about two years until one Sunday, when my pastor gave a particularly scathing sermon on the "sin" of homosexuality. I realized then that the church's view of God was not aligned with my experience of this unconditionally loving, non-judgmental being I had come to know for myself. I decided to step away from the church and allow my soul to lead.

I'm truly grateful for the spiritual support, strength,

and love I gained through the church. Coming together to worship, explore life's mysteries, and find deeper meaning led me to the realization that God is not outside of us. We are all Divine Consciousness, and our relationship with God is our relationship with our Infinite Self, and our power as creators.

Ironically, it was at the height of my born-again Christian experience that I became involved with a married man, Robert. It was a soul connection that overrode all my conditioning around what is "right" and "wrong," and that adultery is a "sin." My mind and my heart were at complete odds, which created an internal conflict that kept me on a wild emotional roller coaster ride for the next five years.

The love we shared was unlike anything I had ever experienced. That relationship brought fun, joy, and laughter into my life. It let the light in. I prayed fervently for God to help me understand how something that felt so good could be so "wrong." The love I experienced in that relationship would be a key part of my inner healing and liberation. I started to question much of the societal rules we blindly follow around relationships. I began to release my judgment of people who have affairs and, eventually, found compassion for myself.

You might find this hard to believe, but there was a gift for my ex-lover and his wife, Serena, in this experience, too.

The day when Serena turned up at my office, I had broken up with Robert, again. He and I had been "on-again, off-again" for five years. During that time, I prayed for the strength to let go of this relationship so that I could find someone who was free to be with me.

As Serena and I made our way to the hotel coffee shop, it dawned on me—this was the answer to my prayer! I just knew there would be no going back now.

Serena looked as nervous as I did. I felt grateful that the coffee shop was not too crowded. Being the empath that I am, I could palpably feel her sadness and fear, and her desperation to know the truth. My heart softened and I felt less guarded.

We talked for over an hour and I answered her questions honestly—something Robert had never done when she had confronted him in the past about her suspicions that he was having affairs.

I felt deep shame and sadness as I acknowledged the role I had played in her husband's betrayal of their marriage vows. I also felt relieved to no longer carry the burden of this secret. Serena, while being understandably angry and hurt, was also relieved because she now had proof of what she had intuitively known for years: she was *not* crazy, and her suspicions were *not* unfounded. She was deeply hurt and yet grateful at the same time.

Robert, on the other hand, was livid when I called him afterward to tell him about our encounter. "What did you tell her?" he asked, his voice full of shock and fear.

"The truth," I said simply.

You know that verse, "The truth will set you free"? It can. And it does.

In this case it cemented the end of our affair and set the stage for the healing of their relationship. It gave Robert an opportunity to stop the hiding and the lies and allowed them to begin to have the difficult, honest conversations they had never had. This ultimately strengthened their marriage, and they are still happily married today.

So much of our pain is caused by our negative judgment of a situation or ourselves, not the actual event itself. The truth really *can* set you free. And as my friend Penny always says, "But first it will piss you off!"

My desire for self-growth and healing led me to the work of Louise Hay. Always an avid reader, I often browsed the airport bookstores to pass time when I traveled. The big, colorful heart on the cover of Louise's book *You Can Heal Your Life* caught my eye in a bookstore in Miami Airport, but I bought it because of the title. I desperately wanted to heal my life!

Truly, when the student is ready, the teacher appears. That was the book that first introduced me to some pivotal concepts and ideas that would become the foundation of my personal transformation and liberation—and is integral to what I still practice and teach today.

I learned that we could transform our lives—our reality, our experiences, even the state of our health—by changing our thoughts and beliefs. I also learned that childhood experiences profoundly shape what we believe about ourselves and the world, and deeply impact what we create, attract, and achieve.

It was then that I realized how I needed to unlearn the beliefs that caused me to see myself as powerless, less than, unworthy, and unlovable; so that I could reconnect with the truth of who I am as a sovereign being and learn to love and accept myself unconditionally.

This new information ignited a profound awakening within me. My life shifted so much that I decided to become certified to facilitate Louise's "You Can Heal Your Life" workshops, so I could share this gift with others. I also had the good fortune of being in the last class of students that got to spend a day with Louise at her home in La Jolla, California during our training. It is a memory I will always cherish.

A few years later I met Tim, the cousin of a good friend. Tim practiced a healing technique called CranioSacral Therapy (CST). I had never heard of it, so I booked a session to experience it for myself.

The treatment involved lying on a massage table, fully clothed. Tim lightly placed his hands on different parts of my body, starting at my feet and progressively moving toward my head. Initially, as he sat touching my feet,

I started to feel a discomfort in my lower back, which eased once his hands went there, but then I started to get a headache.

I lay there feeling agitated, thinking, *I thought this thing was supposed to make you feel good!* Instead, it was bringing up physical pain I didn't have before!

I felt an instinctive urge to resist the pain by tensing up. I wanted to blame Tim for causing the pain. I breathed deeply and tried to relax into the experience.

Instead of judging the pain as "bad" or "wrong," or being angry at Tim, I chose to be curious about what I was feeling and why. This allowed me to relax, stay present, and move through the experience.

Negative judgments and biases cause us to reject, pull back from, and take us out of full presence and connection with what's happening in the moment. Curiosity, on the other hand, embraces, asks a question, and is open. It allows us to stay present with what's happening without needing to judge it. This is really helpful in allowing us to embrace a new experience long enough to form our own opinion of it—and often be delightfully surprised!

By the time Tim got to my head, it felt like the top of my head opened and all the heaviness and pain poured out. After the session, I felt light, clean, and happy—a feeling that lasted not just days, but several weeks.

I wanted to learn how to do that! I wanted to give people the intense relief I experienced, and correct underlying imbalances in the body *before* they become dis-ease.

Within a few years I completed the CranioSacral Therapy and SomatoEmotional Release (SER) training with the Upledger Institute. The theory behind this therapeutic technique is that unresolved emotional and physical trauma can cause dysfunction and pain in the body. If at the time of the physical or emotional trauma we are unable to process and resolve it, the body will wall off the affected area with an electromagnetic field to form an energy cyst.

Energy cysts can interfere with the flow of energy and fluid through the tissues of the body—like a boulder placed in the middle of a stream. They disrupt and sometimes redirect the flow of energy, blood, and lymph, and can impact the body's healing processes and optimal functioning. Unfortunately, X-rays, CAT scans, and MRIs do not pick up energy cysts.

The information I learned in the classes, and the personal healing I received when we practiced with each other, opened up my mind to a whole new level of possibilities regarding healing and the mind-body connection.

I witnessed over and over how the tissues of the body mirror our state of mind and respond to our beliefs: how our emotional state and our mindset impacts the state of the physical body and its functions. Have you ever felt a knot of fear in your stomach, or had the breath knocked out of you by sudden shock? That's what I'm talking about.

One of the most impactful demonstrations of this was a patient I had while working in the outpatient physical therapy department at a hospital. Jenny came seeking relief from severe neck, back, hip, and leg pain. She had sustained multiple fractures many years before in a fall from a second-story building, and although those physical injuries had long since healed, she still suffered from chronic pain related to them.

As we began her treatment, Jenny's physical pain began to ease–however, she started to unravel mentally. I came to find out that her recent bout of physical pain had started during a three-month stay in a local psychiatric hospital. She had a clinical diagnosis of multiple personality disorder. The method of treatment was a combination of medication and teaching her to cope and function by repressing her traumatic memories. The downside of this was that these memories simply became lodged in her tissues and now expressed themselves as extreme physical pain.

As we released the energy from the physical tissues, the emotional pain came to the surface. While we worked to strengthen her muscles and create a physical foundation of support, I taught Jenny how to mentally hold space for her physical and emotional pain from a place of acceptance, compassion, and non-judgment. I taught her to access and trust the wisdom of her "Inner Physician"–the infinite part of her that has the wisdom, knowledge, and understanding of her unique path to healing.

Being a strong believer in Christianity, Jenny developed her own visualization that she would do whenever she felt overwhelmed or out of control. She would imagine herself in a beautiful garden with all the "children" sitting at the feet of Jesus. (The "children" represented the fragmented parts of herself that her psyche had created as a brilliant way to cope and survive the horrific traumas of her early life.) This would instantly calm her and bring her back to feeling grounded, centered, and at peace.

Over time, Jenny learned to be with and process her feelings instead of repressing them and holding them in her body. Her episodes of fragmenting were fewer, and she was generally happier and healthier. She went on to meet and marry a man within a year, and the last time we spoke, Jenny was living happily with her new love.

As my mind opened, I began to approach my patients differently. What if the *root cause* of a physical pain was not necessarily a physical injury? Experiences with clients like Jenny caused me to become more holistic in my approach, more considerate of the mental, emotional, and spiritual issues that may be contributing to my clients' pain.

Even more interesting, I was beginning to understand how we are impacted by the mental and emotional states and energy of *other* people, and how we can take on their pain as our own. How I, as an empath, had taken on and was carrying so much of other people's pain. This is an area not typically addressed in the professional training of healthcare professionals.

This key insight opened the way for me to release so much of the pain I had been carrying, and as I did, I felt increasingly lighter, happier, and freer! This is the power and purpose of acknowledging and healing pain—whether it's on a physical, mental, emotional, or spiritual level.

If that's what you desire, keep reading.

CHAPTER 3

REAWAKENING

I exit the bus coughing and feeling short of breath. The rising panic within me is somewhat relieved when I see Connie in the hotel lobby chatting with two other women.

I walk over to them, my eyes wide, urgent, pleading, and sputter, "Prednisone."

"It's in my room. Come!" Connie says.

The other two women and Connie immediately begin using acupressure to stimulate specific points on my chest and arms. We move as one unit, into and out of the elevator, along the hallway and into Connie's room. They only stop long enough for me to swallow the prednisone with a glass of water.

"I have to lie down," I manage to whisper as a wave of exhaustion pours over me. They follow me to the bed. I am unable to open my eyes, but I am aware of the sensation of energy pouring from their hands into my body.

Suddenly, I find myself looking down at my body on

the bed, surrounded by these caring women. I hear one woman, Maureen, ask, “Helen, where are you?”

“I’m above you,” I reply matter-of-factly.

“Just don’t go too far,” she instructs me.

I had arrived in Beijing tired and stressed from managing Dad’s end-of-life care and handling the funeral arrangements. While all of this was going on, my business was growing exponentially, and I continued to engage in continuing professional education. I came to China for a three-week medical massage training at the Guang’anmen Hospital.

A week into our program, a master acupuncturist was scheduled to give a presentation to the group at our hotel. I had come down with a cold that gradually worsened over the first week, and I was not feeling well. After we got back from class at the hospital that day, I decided to take a nap, asking my roommate, Maria, to wake me before the session.

When Maria woke me, I was running a fever but went to the seminar anyway. I didn’t want to miss an opportunity to learn from one of the last living acupuncture masters who hand-made instruments.

The interpreter had not yet arrived, so I lay down on a bed in the suite where we were all gathered. I felt weak.

Connie, a member of the group who was also a physical therapist, asked how I was doing. I was so short of breath that I couldn't even finish a sentence. Connie recognized I was having an asthma attack. She tried to ask the teacher to help me, but he spoke no English and the interpreter had not yet arrived. We simply had to wait.

Barely breathing, I lay quietly on the bed, unable to even keep my eyes open. I knew I was dying. It was surreal. I was not afraid. My thoughts wandered from worrying that my mom would have the hassle of getting my body from China back to Jamaica, to feeling grateful for the quality time spent with family and friends who attended my dad's funeral a week earlier.

The interpreter finally arrived amidst a flurry of chatter and laughter. Desperate to get her attention, Connie shouted, "She's *dying* over here!", effectively bringing silence to the room. Connie then insisted that she tell the teacher, who was about to start his lecture, that he needed to treat me immediately.

The master teacher worked quickly, inserting acupuncture needles into different points on my body. The effect was profound and rapid. Fifteen minutes later, I was able to breathe without difficulty. We were all amazed. The fact that the members of the group witnessed this would come in handy only a few days later, when I had another attack.

"If you feel another attack coming on, come find me," Connie had told me, explaining that she had prednisone and would give me some if I needed it.

After leaving my body, I found myself moving through a red, mesh-like tunnel and then floating above a big, bright city. I thought it was New York City, but I realized it was actually Shanghai from when we visited there the following week.

Shocked and confused, I just as quickly found myself back in my body, observing vivid images scrolling like film clips on a screen that was the back of my eyelids.

I observed scenes from many different lifetimes when I had lived in China: walking my pet bird with the bamboo cage suspended at the end of a pole, being a concubine in the Forbidden City, boiling potions as a healer ...

Then, I saw myself hovering over a simple white house and instantly felt the weight of deep emotional pain in my heart. I saw myself walk into the forest behind the house. I *knew* I had left my child there and I had not returned. I had killed myself. In that moment I realized the deep pain I was feeling in my heart was what my child had felt when I abandoned him.

The pain felt unbearable. I opened my eyes to try to make it stop. Thankfully, it did.

Maureen, who had been gently massaging a point in the center of my chest over the heart chakra, began speaking softly to me, channeling a message from Spirit about me needing to love and accept my son unconditionally—that all he needed was my love. As she spoke, it dawned on me that the message was about my oldest son, Matthew, and that he was the child I had left behind in that lifetime.

As my strength returned, I sat up with the help of the ladies who had spontaneously stepped in to support me, hold me, and keep me alive. They were truly my angels that day. Later, I asked how they had known that I had left my body. How did Maureen know to ask me where I was? They all replied in unison, "Your body went ice cold!"

The message Maureen brought through profoundly changed my relationship with my son, Matthew. When Matthew was four years old, I found him wearing my mother's silky nightgown, spinning with delight. I sharply reprimanded him. He was just a child playing but, in that moment, I had a glimpse of who he truly was. My fear caused me to instantly block the insight I had in that moment–that he was gay, just like my father.

It was a painful realization. I started to see how, over the years, I had been *unconsciously* rejecting who Matthew really was. I had gone to great lengths, including oral surgery and speech therapy, to help him overcome his natural lisp, and I chastised him whenever he crossed his legs "like a girl." My heart ached with this realization, but it created the opportunity to change my relationship with Matthew.

This near-death experience also reawakened my empathic abilities, which I had repressed as a child in an attempt to "fit in." At that time, I often questioned my sanity because I saw or heard things that others didn't.

I frequently heard footsteps in the house at night, the rocking chair creaking, or the pages of a newspaper being shuffled. I was terrified, but in an effort to prove to myself that I was not imagining things, I made myself look out the window above my bed. I saw the chair rocking all by itself and there was no newspaper in sight. I knew it wasn't the wind causing the chair to move because the leaves of the huge fern beside it were perfectly still.

I felt different and misunderstood, so for many years I disconnected from this part of myself and judged it as strange, weird, and undesirable. The further I stepped away from the truth of who I was, the more I negatively judged myself and denied my innate abilities—and the more lost I felt.

I truly believe this lack of self-love, and the disconnection it created from my true self, was at the root of my depression. I have come to think of depression as a form of emotional pain whose purpose is to awaken us when we are not honoring or expressing our deepest truths and desires, or when we are believing a lie to be true. It invites us to uncover and change the perspectives that cause us to judge, shame, or blame ourselves and others.

As I embraced my authentic self, my intuitive abilities strengthened. As I learned to love and accept all aspects of myself, releasing judgment of myself and others, and speaking my truth with love, I became more clear, courageous, and confident. I was reclaiming my power, and my relationships, health, and finances blossomed!

I began to understand the role that pain plays in showing us where something is misaligned, and in guiding us home to being our most authentic and whole self—the unique gift we came to be in this world—so that we can experience our greatest joys and desires, live our highest potential, and reclaim our power.

I started to share these insights with my clients as I worked with them, helping them to embrace the opportunity that pain presents and make it their ally, instead of the enemy.

As I helped clients make this shift in their perspective, they would get relief faster and it would last longer! It was particularly effective with patients who had not gotten any relief from traditional therapeutic modalities alone. It took me a while to figure out what I was doing intuitively, but eventually I would define, and refine, the step-by-step process I will share with you in the next part of the book.

Whether the source of your pain is "obvious" to you or not, if it doesn't go away or keeps coming back, it means you haven't gotten to the *real* issue—the root problem.

This is why you cannot ignore your pain. If you learn to "live with it," you will stop looking for answers and close the door on new insights and possibilities. It's easy to ignore and dismiss less intense pain. Some emotional states may not *feel* painful, but do not ignore them. Maybe there's a low-level anxiety that lurks just beneath the surface of your skin, an unrelenting tension in your neck and shoulders, a knot in your stomach, or a sadness that dampens your ability to enjoy your beautiful life. And if you are empathic or intuitive, like me, you may feel some form of pain on a near-constant basis due to your heightened sensitivity to your surroundings.

Acknowledge the presence of the pain, whether it is a physical sensation or an emotional issue, or both, and accept that it is a problem for you. Then, make a decision to change it. Many people get stuck in the "land of indecision" because the mind wants to know how you're going to change things before it's willing to act. You can choose to be curious about how the pain might be here to serve you in some way. This requires opening your mind to looking at old things in a new way.

Your commitment is key, because it is the fuel that will keep you moving forward when things get uncomfortable or when you get distracted. While most of us can focus for a short period of time, *sustaining* the focus until we achieve our goal is where we often fail.

Habitual thoughts, feelings, and behaviors are entrenched like well-worn railway tracks in our brains. Consistency and focus are required to deepen the new tracks we are creating through the process of change.

Commitment is sticking to a decision you have made by repeatedly getting back on track each time you slip out of your new behavior—the shallow, new groove in your brain—into the old behavior, your default programming.

I invite you to commit to taking this short and powerful journey with me in this book. In the end, you will have a proven road map that guides you in shifting from pain to peace and having the clarity, courage, and confidence to transform your life.

Are you committed to making a shift? You are so worth it.

Let's go.

PART II

THE SHIFT SYSTEM™ FOR TRANSFORMATION

There is a simple 5-step system I have developed to help you break the cycle of pain. Whether the pain you are experiencing is physical, mental, emotional, or spiritual, releasing it begins by being willing to make a SHIFT.

As I said in the previous chapter, you have to decide that you want something to be different and be willing to *do* something about it. This may require taking different actions, releasing old habits that are not serving you, changing your point of view, and opening up to possibilities you have not previously considered.

Clearly on some level you are ready for this, or you would not be reading this book!

The SHIFT System™ for transforming pain to peace is as follows:

S **See and Surrender.** Acknowledge the pain or discomfort that is present.

H **Honor.** Release any judgment of the pain or yourself for having it.

I **Identify.** Recognize the message the pain brings and how it is here to serve you.

F **Focus and Feel.** Focus on what you want. Feel what's true for you.

T **Take Transformative Action.** Take action based on the messages you receive.

CHAPTER 4

STEP 1: SEE AND SURRENDER

One of the nurses in the hospital where I worked, Kay, had been referred to me for physical therapy following a knee operation. She was not doing her exercises, which was slowing the progress of her rehabilitation and healing.

Kay told me she had undergone the same surgery on her other knee a few years earlier. She remembered experiencing a great deal of pain with the exercises and so she was reluctant to do them. The problem was that she was afraid of experiencing the pain. She hadn't attempted them again, so she actually didn't know how they would feel this time.

Like so many of us, Kay's mind was using a past experience to make assumptions about her current reality. This is how we inadvertently create undesirable outcomes for ourselves. If she was going to have a different experience, I'd have to help her see things differently. We'd need to shift her mindset.

I used an energy psychology technique with her called tapping, or Emotional Freedom Technique (EFT). This involves tapping on specific acupuncture points on the upper body while addressing the issue. I had Kay imagine herself doing her exercises and rate the level of fear she felt. It was a 10/10!

I told Kay to mirror what I did and said as I began to tap on the outside edge of one hand with the tips of the fingers of the other. "Even though I'm afraid of feeling the same pain I had after my last knee surgery, I deeply and completely love and accept myself."

"Even though I'm afraid to feel pain, so I don't do my exercises, I accept that's how I feel, and I'm open to having a different experience this time."

We tapped on the inner edge of the eyebrows and said: "This fear of the pain."

Then, tapping on the side of the eyes: "Releasing this fear of the pain."

Tapping gently on the cheekbones, just under the eyes: "I give my body permission to relax."

Tapping under the nose above the lip: "All this fear of feeling pain with my exercises."

Tapping between the bottom lip and the chin: "Releasing this fear of the pain."

Tapping under the collarbone: "All this fear of the pain."

Tapping on the side of the chest, just below the armpits: "Releasing this fear of the pain."

Finally, on the top of the head: "I give my body permission to relax and let go of this fear of feeling the pain."

I could see Kay's whole body begin to relax, and she took a spontaneous, deep breath. She could now imagine herself doing the exercises without any anxiety.

With her fear of the pain reduced to 0/10, Kay was willing to do her exercises consistently. Her discomfort was surprisingly minimal. She improved rapidly and was discharged from physical therapy and back to work within two weeks!

The first step in the process of change is to see and really become aware of where you are and what you feel, because you can't change what you can't see. This is the biggest way that pain serves us: by making us aware there is a problem asking to be addressed.

This first step is the most important one. It is the starting gate to resolving the problem. Your awareness and acknowledgment of the problem activates the receiving of the gift it brings. If you skip this step, you run the risk of going on a wild goose chase, getting stuck, staying in pain, or even exacerbating the pain.

This step requires self-awareness and being fully present in your body. This means surrendering to the present moment, connecting with it, and being present with what *is*—not what you *wish* it was.

Sounds simple enough, right? But it can be challenging. Most of us have learned to fear feeling our pain, so we avoid facing and feeling it in an attempt to cope and survive.

We have to feel it to heal it. And with the right tools and support, the process can be much easier and faster than you might imagine.

TRY THIS EXERCISE

Take a few moments right now and connect with yourself by putting one hand on your chest and the other on your lower belly. (Seriously, put this book down if you need to.) Take a deep breath. Then, take another slow, deep breath, and notice what is present.

What sensations do you feel? Pause and check in.

What thoughts are running through your mind?

What emotions are present?

Notice any tension or discomfort. Imagine sending the breath there while saying: "I see you, I feel you. Thank you for showing yourself to me. I am willing to understand why you are here and what gifts you may have for me."

We don't just see with our physical eyes. We "see" with all our senses. Seeing refers to awareness: becoming aware of what is going on both within you and around you, what you are thinking, feeling, or sensing.

If you're reading this book, chances are you are a highly sensitive person. Many sensitive or empathic people shut down or dampen their sensitivity as a way of coping. It can feel overwhelming to perceive so much energy and information, and the nervous system can shut down in order to protect itself. This directly impacts your level of self-awareness.

My client Inga had great difficulty feeling anything—physically or emotionally. She felt ashamed to admit this for a long time. She couldn't "see" anything in her mind's eye when we did guided visualizations. She couldn't feel sensations when we did body awareness exercises. Inga thought she was weird, wired differently. She figured she just wasn't a "touchy-feely" person, but secretly, it really bothered her. She really wanted to connect with her body and heal herself of a myriad of medical conditions. Inga was in deep physical, mental, emotional, and spiritual pain.

As we worked together, Inga began to strengthen her connection to her body. She learned to perceive and trust the signals it was giving her. It turned out that she is actually very sensitive and intuitive but, as a result of being abused as a child, she had shut down emotionally in order to survive. Inga is still on her healing journey but is unrecognizable when compared to her former self. She went from being in constant physical pain and emotionally distant, to living pain free most of the time and being able to express her emotions. Inga takes far less pain medication, is physically able to exercise, and is no longer on hyper-alert, micromanaging her children's lives from a place of constant fear.

Seeing is about tuning into, and learning how to be with, the energy and information you perceive and using it to inform you and guide you. Physical sensations are your body's feedback mechanism, as are emotions. Sometimes what you may sense is not visible to the naked eye, so learning to acknowledge and trust these subtle energies around and within you, and accepting them instead of dismissing them, is key to tapping into your inner guidance system and letting it serve you powerfully.

TRY THIS EXERCISE

Stand or sit still and look straight ahead. Notice what you see. Turn your body 45 degrees to the right. Now what do you see? Notice there are things in your field of vision that you did not see before and things you could see before that you now cannot. Notice that this small change in the angle you are looking at something from—your perspective—can create a huge change in what you see.

Some popular ways to expand your self-awareness are meditation, mindfulness, yoga, journaling, and massage. Have you ever been for a massage because your neck was tight and when the therapist touched other parts of your body you were surprised how tight or painful they were? Yet you hadn't been aware of this before they were touched, right?

Some people are afraid that if they acknowledge their pain, it will make it more real. It will make it "stick." But to chart your course, you have to know where you are starting from and where you want to end up. If you don't acknowledge where you are, your inner guidance can't help you. You can't get clear directions from point A to point B if you are pretending you are at point C.

Once you have seen where you are and acknowledged what you are feeling, then you must surrender. Stop fighting and resisting what you are feeling and experiencing. This stops their flow and will keep you stuck where you are.

Surrender is about learning to relax *into* the pain. You might be thinking, *What? Relax and pain in the same sentence?!* I know it sounds counterintuitive. Just trust me on this.

By consciously embracing and relaxing into the pain, you help to release it.

Seeing without surrendering makes the process of change one of struggle versus ease. In surrendering, you release the handbrake of resistance, and you are once again in the flow. There is movement of breath, blood, lymph, and energy, allowing for healing to occur. New ideas, solutions, and perspectives can also flow in.

I'm going to also invite you to surrender the idea that you know the cause of your pain, no matter how "obvious" it may seem. You might think that it is because you lifted that heavy box, or because your spouse cheated, or because you had shoulder surgery two weeks ago. While you may be absolutely correct, that information may be blocking you from getting deeper insight about the pain and the gifts it has for you.

Monica, a long-standing client of mine, showed up for her life coaching session with a raging headache. She explained it was because she'd had a minor surgery the day before to remove two cysts from her scalp. She assumed that was the source of her headache the next day.

My gut told me otherwise, so I worked with Monica and took her through the SHIFT process in this book.

I asked her to take a few deep breaths, close her eyes, get present, and notice what came into her awareness.

She became aware of the tension in her muscles and a tightness in her jaw.

Monica remembered that her sister had called earlier to complain about the hotel reservations she had made for the family reunion over the Thanksgiving holiday.

She acknowledged her growing anxiety around having invited her mom to the Thanksgiving get-together. Monica was regretting inviting her mom, as she was sure that there would be drama between her and the other invited guests.

I asked why she thought that would be so. "My mom is so judgmental! She is a very opinionated Christian and makes disparaging comments to people about their choices and lifestyle. She is going to offend someone—I just know it!"

I gently pointed out that she was judging her mother right now, and that she was stressing herself out, trying to control a situation that hadn't even happened yet.

Monica began to see that she was creating the pressure and stress by imagining a worse-case scenario.

We tapped to release the judgment: "Even though I am judging my mom right now, I deeply and completely accept myself anyway."

"Even though I'm stressing myself out about something that hasn't happened yet, I deeply and completely love and accept myself."

"Even though I don't believe things can be peaceful if my mom is there ..."

Monica began to cry as a memory surfaced in her mind. She was around six years old and was wanting her mom to make her feel safe. Her mom was emotionally unavailable, and Monica was still carrying that hurt and pain. *This* was the root issue that wanted to be acknowledged and released.

I had Monica imagine herself holding her six-year-old self and giving her the love and support that her mother couldn't give her at the time. As she did, the tension in her body released and her headache subsided.

Monica then imagined a different scenario for the upcoming Thanksgiving gathering—one aligned with the outcome she desired versus the stressful scenes she was previously imagining. The result was an enjoyable, drama-free Thanksgiving family reunion a few days later!

You have to be willing to let go of where you are so you can get to where you want to be. This can be difficult because the mind can create sophisticated defense mechanisms to protect itself and keep you "safely" in your comfort zone—no matter how dysfunctional it might be. These protective "guards" are created from fear, past experiences, or observations of others. They stem from a belief that you are not safe. And while that may have been true at some point in your life, chances are it's not true anymore.

Most of the time the *idea* of feeling the pain is actually scarier than the reality of it, which is exactly what happened with Kay. The key to her rapid results was that we were able to identify, acknowledge, and then address the *real* problem—now. This is the starting point of making any change, and it is often where people get hung up. As they say, denial is not just a river in Egypt!

So starting with what you are actually feeling and experiencing right now is key. You already have the most amazing tool for doing this—your breath! Conscious breathing is a powerful way to bring yourself to the present moment and to release and manage pain. This is why pregnant women are taught to breathe through their labor pains.

Your breathing automatically changes when you are in physical pain or emotionally upset. It usually becomes faster and shallower, further activating the stress response in your body. Consciously changing your breathing pattern can deactivate your sympathetic nervous system, which controls "fight, flight, or freeze," and activate your parasympathetic nervous system, which controls "rest and repair." It is a powerful way to shift your pain, become more present, and calm yourself.

TRY THIS EXERCISE

Take a deep belly breath. Fill your lungs with as much air as they can hold. When you are full, hold your breath in. Keep holding your breath but relax your muscles. Take another sip of air in through your mouth. Hold it. Relax your body again. Keep holding your breath and relaxing your body. When you can't hold your breath any longer, release it. Feel the release of tension in your body.

Repeat the process again and notice any changes in the amount of air you can take in and how long you can hold your breath. It is always interesting to note any fearful thoughts you may have while holding your breath.

The average person breathes fifteen to twenty times every minute. With every exhalation you have another opportunity to practice letting go.

If you did that exercise, you should be feeling a little calmer right now, so let's look at a few more important things that we need to consider letting go of if we want to make this journey easier.

We also need to surrender our attachments. These are mental ideas and perspectives that keep us hanging on to things, people, places, and behaviors that are no longer useful or relevant. They limit our possibilities and keep us stuck when our true nature is to continually expand and evolve.

Here are some common attachments we have:

To a particular outcome: *That should not have happened!*

To how we are seen or perceived by others: *He will be upset if I don't come.*

To having the "right" answers: *Of course. I knew that!*

Every time we say or think "I know that," the brain stops being open to finding out more. Because you have "the answer," it stops looking for other solutions or possibilities.

I was raised in a family that valued being smart and I was rewarded for having the right answers. Being highly educated, skillful, nice, and generous is what made me feel worthy. I wasn't taught I had inherent value for simply being myself, so I spent much of my life proving I was worthy and earning the love, appreciation, and trust I craved by being the good girl, toeing the line, and stuffing my anger. Can you relate to this?

I've had to surrender this attachment because I've come to see how it zaps my energy and my joy, and actually creates pain.

What does it take to actually surrender? It takes trust. And that, my friend, is the crux of the matter. We have to surrender the guards or protective barriers that we created when we were injured or didn't feel safe.

When the muscles around a musculoskeletal injury contract to stabilize the area in an attempt to support it and prevent further injury, we call it "splinting." However, this splinting also puts pressure on the blood vessels and nerves in the area and can impact the flow of blood and lymph that carry the very things the tissues need to heal.

When we excitedly or vulnerably share something dear to our heart with someone and they criticize or dismiss it, we shield our heart and vow "never again." This can actually create an energetic wall around our heart that can impact our ability to connect deeply with others in the future, and even with ourselves.

We must also be willing to surrender any self-judgment, blame, and shame in order to become a safe space for ourselves. This creates a deeper connection with yourself, which leads to further self-awareness.

We also have to surrender the idea that we are powerless and that letting go is "giving up" or a sign of weakness. Many people balk at the idea of surrendering. Technically, it is the ego mind that resists the idea. This is about surrendering to the heart and soul.

In spending our most formative years in traditional educational institutions, the mind has been given the power to lead, but it does *not* have all the answers. It only recreates what it already knows—what it has learned through education, experience, or observation, so it cannot readily take you into the expansiveness of the not-yet-known.

Your mind has to be willing to surrender to your soul and collaborate with your heart in service to the soul. The good news is that your soul has been in control all along and has conspired on your behalf with your body and mind to get you here. This book did not end up in your hands by chance.

I invite you to surrender and choose to trust the part of you that got you here. It's safe to explore something new. You can always change your mind later. For now, take a breath, relax, and let's take the next step together.

CHAPTER 5

STEP 2: HONOR

"Helen!" my mother screams from across the room. It shocks me back into presence. My vision clears and I gasp. I am sitting on top of my five-year-old brother, Andrew, my hands around his throat, squeezing the very life out of him—his lips are blue and his eyes are wild with terror. Horrified, I let go and he gasps for air.

"What are you doing?" Her face mirrors the horror, confusion, and fear I am feeling myself. "What's *wrong* with you?"

My twelve-year-old self had no clue, so I couldn't really explain it to her, or anyone else.

While I can't specifically recall what Andrew did or said that day that caused me to react so violently, I do know

I experienced what is called *blind rage*—anger that is so consuming that one becomes blind to other people and to logic. I was staring into his face *but not seeing him*—completely unaware of what I was doing. If Mom hadn't entered the room when she did, Andrew could have died. I shudder as I think of this even now, all these years later.

Looking back from the vantage point of hindsight wisdom, I realize it wouldn't have taken much for me to explode. Yes, Andrew was a typical annoying little brother—wanting to hang out in our bedroom, playing pranks, like hiding my sister's engagement ring, to get attention—but there was also a low-grade anxiety and anger that had been simmering within me for years. I hated the sense of powerlessness I felt as a child, not having control over what I ate and when, where I went to school, who I got to play with, or how I expressed myself.

I didn't realize it at the time, but the deepest wound this violent incident created was the way it negatively impacted my relationship with myself. I saw myself as crazy, unpredictable, and out of control. It undermined my trust in myself and my ability to control my big emotions. It also cemented my greatest fear—that something *was* wrong with me. I became afraid of my sensitive, emotional self. I learned to judge and hate this part of me, which caused me to resist and repress it further. I vowed I would never get that angry again.

The challenge with any form of negative judgment is that it creates separation and disconnection. It breeds shame, blame, and excuses; and causes us to rationalize, justify, and defend. These actions and reactions are based in fear, not love. We need love to heal. We need connection to heal.

Emotional pain that is unaddressed or repressed only grows. It will eventually erupt and can wreak havoc and destruction that could have been prevented.

I would eventually take myself to therapy as an adult to try to understand why I was so angry and learn healthy ways to express my feelings, but it was something my second husband, Gary, taught me many years later that would truly liberate me. He said: "You don't need to explain, rationalize, or justify what you are feeling, Helen. Your feelings are simply your feelings. It doesn't matter *why* you are feeling them."

This powerful insight blew my mind. I had grown up always having to defend my feelings: "*Why are you so . . . [sad, happy, angry, upset, or fill in the blank]*?" This realization became the basis for Step 2 of the SHIFT process: Honor.

Honoring means to give great respect. With this step, we are honoring and accepting ourselves and our feelings, without judgment. This is an act of tremendous self-love.

This step requires unlearning, because we have all been taught to judge, that is, to see things as "right" or "wrong" and "good" or "bad." Judgments are learned perspectives that we take on through our education and socialization. As we go through life and become more self-aware, we get to discern and decide what we like or don't like and what we would prefer, then make empowering choices based on our own experiences. This is an important part of owning our power.

Learning not to judge your feelings as "good/bad" or "right/wrong" and to simply accept them is so freeing. Releasing the need to stop and justify, rationalize, or explain your emotions, or "understand" and "figure out" why you feel the way you feel in that very moment, allows the energy to keep flowing.

It's also important to take the time to reflect on and process your emotions. Remember, your feelings, even the painful ones, are an important part of your inner guidance system, giving you information and feedback. They must first be acknowledged, accepted, and honored.

Over time, I learned to acknowledge what I was feeling without any need to judge, rationalize, or explain why I was feeling that way. I would simply say to myself, "I am feeling [fill in the blank]." I practiced just letting myself "have my feelings." Tapping, which we learned in the previous chapter, was an important tool because the set-up statement is: "Even though I am feeling [fill in the blank], I deeply and completely love and accept myself." Wow! Saying this was challenging, strange, and exhilarating—all at the same time!

As I learned to embrace my feelings, I was learning to embrace *myself*. I was becoming less reactive. More responsive. I felt more in control of myself.

Just because I had a feeling, it didn't mean I had to do

something with it, or about it, at that moment. This gave me the space to simply be with whatever emotions I was feeling. That space is where I was often able to decipher if what I was feeling was mine or someone else's. This is really key, particularly if you are an empath who picks up on other people's emotions and energies.

Emotions are energy in motion—they're *e-motions*. Energy needs to move and flow. When we resist our emotions, by judging or repressing them, because this may not be the "appropriate time or place to have them," they can get stuck and wreak havoc.

TRY THIS EXERCISE

When you are feeling a strong feeling, pause and ask the question, silently or aloud, "Whom does this belong to?" If the feeling is not yours, it will lighten up immediately. You can then say, "Return to sender with consciousness and love."

I learned this helpful tool from Access Consciousness facilitator Rikka Zimmerman.

Not only have we learned to judge our feelings, we have also learned to judge *everything*. Judgment becomes the filter through which we assess actions and interactions with ourselves and others. It's how we view situations and experiences. These learned judgments become ingrained beliefs that shape and influence our perspectives on ourselves, others, and situations. They drive our assumptions, conclusions, and reactions.

This is why the fastest way we can create a change–in how we are feeling or responding to life–is by changing our perspective. And the most powerful way to change our perspective is by releasing judgment.

As the late Dr. Wayne Dyer famously said, "If you change the way you look at things, the things you look at change." In order to release our well-ingrained habit of judging, we have to change the way we look at judgment, or we end up "judging the judge"–in other words, making ourselves bad or wrong when we catch ourselves judging. I recommend having an "interesting" box instead of a "good" or "bad" box for your mind to file experiences and feelings. That way you can just have an experience without needing to judge it either way.

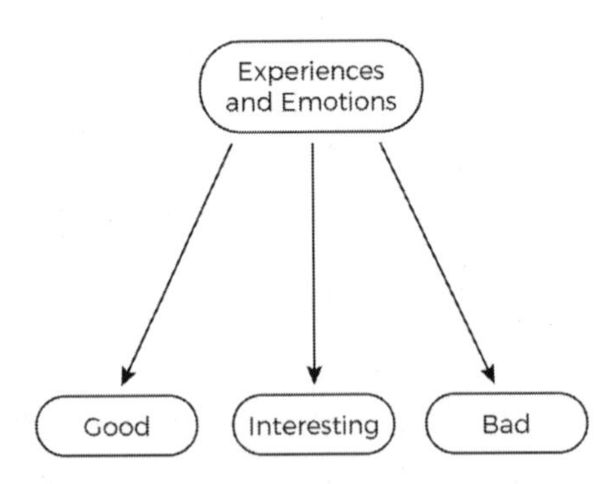

Negative judgment is present whenever we experience pain. We have learned to fear–and resist–that which we judge as "bad" or "wrong" and, as I mentioned earlier, fear creates and exacerbates pain. This is why learning to release judgment is such a healing, freeing, and lifelong practice.

Remember Monica in the previous chapter? Her negative judgment of her mother's behavior was literally creating tension and pain in her body. As I invited her to view her mother's behavior as "interesting," versus "right" or "wrong," it allowed her the space to view her mother and her behavior from a different perspective. Instead, I invited her to be curious about the very things she was judging.

Curiosity asks questions instead of making assumptions. Questions like: "I wonder why ... ?" or "I wonder how ... ?" Curiosity creates an opening, a space, for new, different, and often unexpected perspectives to emerge. It is where we can find compassion, understanding, and connection–the very things our hearts truly desire.

My client Susan was working on releasing judgment. Her increasing self-awareness made her painfully aware of how much she judged herself and others. She was frustrated because she didn't know how to stop.

"I was talking to a young woman at the gym yesterday," she explained. "She told me she ate vegan 90 percent of the time, but as she described what she ate I found myself critiquing her diet choices and comparing them to mine. There was no way she was 90 percent vegan!"

Susan continued. "I realized I was judging her, and immediately felt bad for doing that!"

"So, you were judging the judge," I said.

"Yes! I can't stand my judgmental self. How do I make her go away?"

"You don't," I replied. "You have to embrace her. She just wants to be loved and accepted like every other part of you."

I invited Susan to be curious about how her judgments may actually have served her in some way. She mulled it over for a few minutes. "Well, I suppose it allowed me to feel better about myself as I compared myself to her. She is twenty and I am sixty-five. Her body is fit and toned. It was something I was better at than her."

With this realization, Susan began to feel some compassion for herself and reported feeling a softening throughout her whole body as a result.

TRY THIS EXERCISE

Think of a situation where you are judging yourself or someone else as "wrong" or "bad." Notice how you feel as you think about it, and then write it down. (For example: heavy, angry, frustrated, tense, disappointed.)

Now, let yourself be curious about the impact of your judgment.

Ask yourself:

- I wonder why I/they did/said that?
- I wonder why it bothers me so much?

- I wonder where I learned this?
- I wonder how this might be here to serve me?
- I wonder how I might perceive this situation differently?
- I wonder what I might be afraid of?
- I wonder what it would take to let this go?
- I wonder if I could let myself feel differently?
- I wonder what I'm trying to protect myself from?

Take a few minutes to journal on what comes up as a result of you being curious. Notice how you feel now. What sensations in your body or thoughts in your mind are you now experiencing? Write them down.

It's important to understand the role that releasing judgment plays in expanding your self-awareness and being able to be fully present at any moment..

Being judged feels like a form of attack. It's painful because we don't feel accepted for who we are being. We don't feel safe, so the mind goes into protective mode—putting up guards, managing potential situations—all to ensure our safety. We will lie, pretend, and create distractions to avoid the pain of feeling judged negatively and, as a result, we are not fully present, vulnerable, honest, or authentic. This fuels distrust and disconnection and opens the door for self-judgment. We are often way more judgmental with ourselves than others. We speak to ourselves in our minds in ways we would never dare to speak to anyone else, and treat ourselves with wanton disregard without realizing that we teach people how to treat us as they observe how we treat ourselves. The world serves as a big mirror—with the people and situations that we attract helping us to see ourselves. The less we judge what shows up in the mirror, the more we can embrace the opportunity to evolve, change, and transform our perspective from fear and judgment to love and acceptance.

The more we love and accept ourselves, the more it shows up in the mirror of our lives and we start to find it everywhere we turn. We are more likely to let down our guards and feel safe to engage in a space of non-judgment. As a result we are more present, connected and honest. Less anxious and stressed. We sleep better, and feel lighter and happier. We experience a greater sense of freedom and inner peace. *This* is the power of releasing judgment and practicing self-compassion.

I've experienced this myself, as have the clients I have worked with. As we unlearn to habit of judging ourselves and others, and change our beliefs and perspectives, we change our mindset. We become more sovereign in our thinking and more trusting of what our heart feels and knows. This opens the way for the next step in this process where we identify, and get clarity, on the message the pain has for us.

TRY THIS EXERCISE

To close out this step in honoring our emotions, I invite you to make this powerful declaration for yourself:

I am willing to honor my feelings and my experiences by acknowledging and accepting them without judgment. I am now open to being a safe space for myself, and I use my discernment to guide me in making choices and decisions that are aligned with my greatest joy, freedom, and well-being.

CHAPTER 6

STEP 3: IDENTIFY

I begin my physical therapy assessment by taking a detailed history and asking Sarah what she's feeling—physically and emotionally. She has been having lower back pain on and off for three years, but it's been getting more severe and frequent in the last few months.

As Sarah describes the intense physical discomfort and the movements that exacerbate it, suddenly her face flushes and she looks down, embarrassed. "It's making it almost impossible to have sex, and my husband's family really want us to have a baby."

Sarah begins to cry. I reach over, hold her hand, and gently ask her, "What do *you* want?" She looks up, surprised and somewhat confused, as if no one has ever asked her this question before.

I remind Sarah that, even though she is a married woman, it is still *her* body and she gets to choose whether or not to have children. She tells me how pressured she feels by the societal and familial expectations that she "should" want children–and how guilty she feels for not having the maternal calling so many of her friends seem to have.

"Close your eyes and take a deep breath." I instruct her to put her hands over her heart and guide her through a visualization to connect with her heart and ask it what it wants. Its answer is immediate and very clear–she does *not* want to have children. Sarah sighs spontaneously and her entire body softens as she accepts what she has known to be true in the deepest part of herself. I ask her to check back in with her body, and lo and behold, the pain is completely gone.

Sarah's back pain disappeared without me ever treating her body. There was no need for the traditional therapeutic modalities. We talked about the mind-body connection and her need to communicate her decision with her husband.

Sarah left with instructions to call or come back if the pain returned, but I never heard from her again.

The third step of this process is all about clarity–identifying what the pain is trying to get you to see or do differently. We have to be willing to *confront* what we have been ignoring. After all, there is a reason the pain had to get our attention, right?

In order to confront, embrace, and engage with your pain, it's helpful to remember: *the pain is here for your benefit*. I encourage you to practice choosing this perspective every time. This belief will help you remain open to the process.

Does the idea of confronting anything stop you in your tracks? I used to *hate* confrontation. The very word used to conjure images in my mind of people screaming at each other in a fit of rage, fighting, and hurting each other's feelings. I would avoid it like the plague because I was raised to believe it's "not nice" and I placed a high value on being "nice." Is that true for you, too?

I've come to see that this conditioning is the driving force behind what I call "toxic niceness." This happens when we censor ourselves so much that we hide how we really feel, for fear of hurting someone's feelings or making them upset with us. Toxic niceness causes its own fair share of emotional pain and can cause us to behave inauthentically.

Most people I know tend to avoid confrontation. This is probably because one of its definitions is "to face in hostility or defiance." However, it is also defined as, "to face and deal with boldly or directly," and "to stand or come in front of."

This fear of confrontation causes us to put things outside of our conscious awareness, where we can't see it. This is why it's important for us to reframe what it means to "confront" so it is no longer something we are scared of and try to avoid. Developing this skill can go a long way in allowing our current pain to serve us and eliminating the need for a "blind spot" in which to hide it.

Pause here and check in with yourself. Do you suffer from toxic niceness?

Do you say yes when you really want to say no? Do you love, value, and serve yourself as powerfully as you love, value, and serve others? Or do you find yourself putting your needs and desires on the back burner, and make how other people feel more important than how you feel? Would you rather disappoint yourself before you let yourself disappoint a stranger? Do you often "go along to get along" and acquiesce to keep the peace?

Simply notice what's true for you, without judgment. Remember there is power in acknowledging what is, and this awareness begins the process of change.

Teri hired me to help her resolve the root cause of her pain. She was working hard and yet not achieving the level of success she desired in her business. This left her feeling frustrated and disappointed. Her self-confidence was waning, along with her belief that she would ever accomplish her dream of financial freedom.

Teri had previously created good momentum in her business, reaching a point where she recognized that needed to leave her day job in order to have the time and energy to take on more clients, so that her business could continue to grow. This would require a leap of faith (something we'll talk about more in the next chapter).

Teri set a date to leave her day job—but the date came and went without her taking action. Over the next few months her business started to decline. Several clients did not renew their contracts, and a current client whom Teri was still serving—even though she was three months late on her payments—was off on a European holiday. Teri was left struggling to pay her bills and found herself getting deeper into debt. She was starting to feel deeply resentful.

In order to shift the results she was getting, Teri had to take an honest look at some things *within* herself: Why was it okay to continue to deliver services to a client who owed her three months of payments? Why was she putting a client's needs above her own? And why did she continue to go to a job every day that she *knew* she didn't love?

Teri also had to identify what actions she was willing to take to actualize her big dream, including confronting her fears and the limiting beliefs that were driving them.

Where there is pain, there is fear. To identify what the pain is about, the most powerful question you can ask yourself is: *What am I afraid of?*

The answer that comes to mind first is not always the truest, deepest one. Our greatest fears are often hidden, disguised, or buried deep. Connecting with your body and noticing how it responds to questions can give you insight around this.

The most obvious risk for Teri was leaving her job so she could dedicate more time to her business. The fear was experiencing financial insecurity and having to depend on others for help if she failed.

She also feared putting herself out there and asking people to do business with her. Another fear? Feeling rejected if a potential client said no. As we explored a little deeper, there was the fear of being judged by others for wanting more—fame, success, wealth. There was a belief that it was selfish and greedy to want more, and that nobody else wants to hear that you are doing well. This created a fear of being isolated and alone.

It's important to know that these fears are driven by our beliefs. They are figments of the imagination based on our past experiences, or those of someone else. They are rarely based on truth.

Finally, we identified what it was costing Teri to not take that leap of faith and follow her heart. She was breaking her own heart over and over again. It was creating more pain, disappointment, anxiety, and frustration. Her self-confidence and self-trust were diminished.

I guided her inward, tuning into the place in her body where she was holding this fear. I taught her how to breathe into it and greet it with compassion and acceptance.

Through this process of courageous confrontation, Teri was able to tap into clarity and identify powerful next steps that were aligned with her heart's desires. She was able to collect the money owed to her by the client, and commit to a new date to quit her day job. She also "miraculously" started seeing jobs advertised that were more aligned with what she loved doing, and is ramping up her business again.

When you are out of alignment with your deepest truth, when your fear has you refusing to see the reality of your situation, life will get your attention through pain. It will show up in the places that make it hard to ignore—like your finances, your health, and the relationships that matter to you most.

This pain, which is sometimes mental, emotional, or physical, will give you an opportunity to get back into alignment and experience greater ease, flow, joy, and abundance.

The things we tolerate, or settle for, are a huge source of pain and irritation. Individually, they may seem small, but, collectively, they drain your energy and contribute to the build-up of emotional pain like anger and resentment, as well as physical stress and tension.

TRY THIS EXERCISE

Make a list of ten things that have been irritating you or that you have been "tolerating." For example: the pile of clutter on your bedside table, your employee who is incessantly late, the uncomfortable mattress you sleep on each night, or issues with a loved one you haven't addressed because you don't want to upset them.

(Continued on next page)

Once you have made your list, begin working at resolving them, one at a time. You won't get them all done at the same time, especially if you have a long list, so prioritize the items on your list. Establish a time frame or deadline by which you will have each item done by and start with the ones that are causing you the most pain.

Then, make a separate list of things or people you have been avoiding. (We tend to avoid the things that cause us pain.) Once you've made your list, start with the first item and ask yourself:

- "Why am I avoiding this?"
- "What judgment do I feel about myself or someone else that makes me want to avoid this?"

As we discussed in Chapter 4, we want to release judgment because it is a source of pain. On top of that, our negative judgment of pain creates fear, which only exacerbates pain.

Here's an important tip: we often don't start a task because we overestimate how much time it will take to complete it. Or, we believe we have to complete it all at once. Set a timer for fifteen minutes and start working on one item on your list. I guarantee that you'll be surprised how much you can get done in just fifteen minutes.

Have you noticed how painful it is to *not* have what you want? Perhaps it's a loving relationship, money, freedom, owning a home, or some other goal.

In my years of working with people with this type of pain, I have learned that there are three main reasons people don't have what they want:

1. They haven't taken the time to clearly identify what they want.
2. They haven't taken consistent action toward getting what they want.
3. They don't believe they can have what they want.

Identifying what you want is not always as simple as it sounds because we are conditioned to settle for less than what we want and to make the needs of others a higher priority. Here's how we get around that: first, make a list of what you *don't* want—and why. This will give you insight into what you really want.

Your pain is giving you feedback about what you don't want and telling you that something's not aligned with what you do want. So, some part of you must already know what you want, right? Yes! This is your subconscious mind at work.

You can figure out what you *truly* want, bypassing your conscious, conditioned mind and getting information from your subconscious mind through your body. This is done by accessing your inner yes and no.

TRY THIS EXERCISE

First, think about something you really enjoy—a place, an activity, a person that lights you up and makes you feel really good. Notice the sensations this creates in your body. This is your inner yes.

Next, think about something you really don't like, that you absolutely don't want. Notice how your body feels, reacts, or responds. This is your inner no.

Practice checking in and noticing how your body reacts to different things, places, and people. When you're not sure what you want, ask your body!

Still feeling stuck? Here's yet another way to identify what you want.

TRY THIS EXERCISE

Make a list of what you want to feel. For example: calm, delighted, excited, cherished, accomplished, rich, loved, safe, connected, inspired, energized, engaged, relaxed. Now make a list of the activities, people, things, situations, or places that make you feel these things.

Knowing what you want to feel is important. Think of this list as your North Star guiding you toward what you truly want!

In the next chapter, we're going to dive deeper into engaging with your feelings and how you can let them serve you in a powerful way by honing your focus.

Is life trying to get your attention right now through pain? Have you identified the opportunity that is presenting itself to you?

Wherever, or however, a pain or challenge is showing up, choose to trust that it is here *for* you. It is here for your growth and expansion, for your ultimate benefit, to guide you.

CHAPTER 7

STEP 4: FOCUS

> I'm in a luxurious three-bedroom condo over-looking the ocean. The water is a melody of blue and green hues. The sky is clear and the sun is vibrant. There is a fresh breeze carrying the music from the poolside bar up to the balcony where I sit. I should be feeling calm and happy, but I'm stressed and angry.

Instead of relaxing on the pristine white sand beach with my friends on my Caribbean vacation, I'm up in the condo attending to vital tasks that need to be done for an event we have later in the week, because my assistant has messed up ... again.

I am feeling bitterly disappointed and resentful. My heart is heavy. I'm berating myself for giving her the opportunity to let me down again.

On top of this, we haven't gotten as many people registered as we would have liked for the event. At eleven registrants, we've fallen way short of our goal of fifty, and we worked so hard on it! I feel disheartened and defeated. I am focusing on everything that's going *wrong* and it's making me feel *bad*.

My mood is spiraling downward fast.

I call my business partner, Matthew, to discuss what's happening. My mind is replaying the conversation we had a few weeks earlier when I had told him that I was going to rehire my old assistant. His response was simple and straightforward: "*Why?*" The truth is, I had been feeling desperate at the time. I needed help right away, and she already knew my business.

Thankfully, Matthew is able to quickly and skillfully help me to shift my focus.

He acknowledges my frustration and disappointment and reminds me that we knew the assistant was not the right fit and that it would only be a temporary situation. He then invites me to release my judgment of what was happening and instead *celebrate* the eleven people who have said yes to attending our event. Together, we decide how we want to feel and how we want our attendees to feel: light, happy, and free!

Matthew offers to handle the communication with the assistant so I can join my friends at the beach. I hang up the phone and sigh, feeling light and free.

In Step 1 of this process, we established the importance of seeing the pain for what it is and surrendering to the present moment.

Releasing judgment and honoring your feelings in Step 2 opened the way for clarity and supported your ability to identify what you want in Step 3. Now, in Step 4, you get to focus on what you want, from a place of faith, trusting that you *can* have it.

Focus is paying conscious attention. It is directing your thoughts toward something specific. Like the lens of a camera, we can zoom in or out. We can have a narrow focus where we direct our attention like a laser beam. This is powerful and has its uses at times, especially when we need to eliminate distractions. Or we can zoom out and widen our focus, making it more diffuse. With a wider focus, we can see a wider range of possibilities.

Consciously engaging your focus requires a willingness to be fully present and fully engaged in what is happening with you and your environment in any given moment. When we split our focus through multitasking—giving our attention to more than one thing at the same time—we dilute our presence and our power.

The truth is: multitasking is an illusion. When we are doing two things at the same time, the brain is switching its focus rapidly from one to the other, so it *appears* as though we are focusing on them at the same time. This is important to know so that you don't try to multitask when you are doing something that requires your undivided attention.

To make things more complicated, digital technology has made information even more accessible, and with incredible speed. There are so many things vying for our attention that it can be overwhelming. So how do we maintain a grounded presence and powerful focus without completely disengaging?

Firstly, you have to prioritize. What's most important at this moment? This is why it's so important to clarify what you want in Step 3 of the process. When you are clear about what you want and why it matters, decision-making and prioritizing are much easier!

Next, you can expand your focus—and possibilities—by adopting a "yes, and" approach instead of an "either/or" perspective. Here's an example: "Yes, I would like to spend more time with my family, *and* I need to establish firm boundaries."

This is opposed to a fixed perspective that says: "I can only have this *or* that, not both." Maybe you can't have them both *at the exact same moment*, but in holding space for the *possibility*, your brain will get to work on figuring out how.

As someone who was raised to think in terms of "either/or" or "all-or-nothing" when making choices, learning this "yes, and" perspective allowed my mind to open to possibilities I would never have considered!

This was the case recently, when the final week of a training program I was enrolled in, which had gotten rescheduled due to the pandemic, coincided with a new program we were launching.

I was doing all the administrative work for the launch, and my mind was busy trying to figure out what to do. Matthew asked me a key question: "What does your heart want? What will bring you joy?"

I thought about being at the training program with my fellow trainers and my body felt light and tingled with joy. That's my internal "yes!" The decision was made! I would do both. I didn't know *how* at that moment, but I knew I'd figure it out. And I did. It was easier than I thought, because the training was on the west coast and that gave me three hours in the morning to get things done for my business on the east coast, before starting my training on the west coast.

When you focus on what you love, things have a way of working themselves out. Often our pain is showing us where we are being limited in our thinking, and if we can shift our perspective and focus, the "pain" disappears—without the situation or anyone else having to change. When my clients experience this, it always feels miraculous.

This was the case with my client Peaches, a wife and mother to four children who was living a learned behavior pattern of "do for others before you do for yourself."

"My needs weren't as important as my husband and children," she said. "I kept going until I ran myself into the ground. I was exhausted, miserable, resentful, and angry! I'd see my husband taking time for himself and that made me even angrier!

"I knew if I didn't stop and do something for myself, it

wasn't going to end well. I hit a wall. I couldn't continue to live my life that way. I thought: *There's got to be an alternative.*"

Through our work together, Peaches changed some outdated beliefs that were not aligned with what she wanted to experience. She changed how she approached things. She started acknowledging and communicating her needs and asking for what she wanted. And as she did, she started to feel different.

Now she says, "I'm still doing the same things, but with more joy. I am better able to show up for them when I give to myself. My children are much calmer because I am calmer. In hindsight, I realize that my anger and resentment were creating a typhoon and everyone was caught up in it. When my attitude changed, everyone else did, too. We talk more. I listen now. I pause and listen. I used to think I couldn't be a good mother *and* go after my dreams. I now know that's not true. My husband and children are my biggest cheerleaders now in encouraging me to follow my heart. They love seeing me happy!"

Remember, your feelings are feedback. They show you what you have been focusing on. If you focus on something you judge as "negative," on what you are afraid of, or what you *don't* want, you will usually feel "bad"—unmotivated, hopeless, lost, exhausted, confused, unclear, rejected, or disappointed.

Conversely, when you focus on what you *do* want, you feel "good"—happy, energized, motivated, inspired, connected, clear, focused, peaceful, and loved.

TRY THIS EXERCISE

First, get a piece of paper and draw a line down the middle, creating two columns.

Next, label the left column "I feel." Write down everything you're feeling right now, physically and emotionally, putting each feeling on a separate line.

Label the right column "I would prefer to feel." For every sensation or emotion you listed on the left, write what you would prefer to be feeling instead on the right.

I feel ...	**I would prefer to feel ...**
overwhelmed	calm, organized, focused
anxious	relaxed, peaceful, calm, care-
guilty	free comfortable, self-assured,
ashamed	proud confident, at ease,
angry	supported calm, peaceful,
lonely	content, joyful supported,
poor	connected, loved rich, abun-
jealous	dant, wealthy happy, content,
needy	complete loved, supported,
	cherished, contented

Sometimes you may have difficulty coming up with what you would prefer to feel. If this happens, just imagine what the opposite of the negative feeling might be and describe that.

Once you have completed your list, make a choice to focus on how you would prefer to feel. Notice if any resistance comes up for you in this process. Resistance is a symptom of fear. If you notice it, ask yourself: *What am I afraid of?* Be willing to feel and identify the fear and breathe through it.

Your focus is a powerful tool. Where you focus your attention, your energy goes. Being able to shift your focus is a superb skill to develop because it can change everything on a dime!

In addition to the exercise on the previous page, there are many tools and processes that can help you shift your focus in a powerful and positive way. However, as I've mentioned, one of the greatest challenges when you are in severe pain is being able to focus on anything, much less something positive. In those moments, you may need some outside help.

Eventually, with consistent practice, shifting your focus on how you would like to feel will happen naturally, like how it did with Peaches.

The universal Law of Attraction states that what you focus on expands. It took me a long time to figure out that I wasted so much time and energy focusing on what I *didn't* want.

In school, I learned that being smart was figuring out how to solve problems. My brilliant mind was well trained in focusing on what was "wrong"—which often led to feelings of frustration and negativity, and pretty much guaranteed that there would inevitably be more things to "fix." This is a common challenge many of my clients also have—even the most savvy and successful of them.

Being able to spot and fix problems is a valuable skill set because fixing a problem brings relief. However, this focus inadvertently creates new problems to fix, and we end up in a never-ending pain > relief cycle.

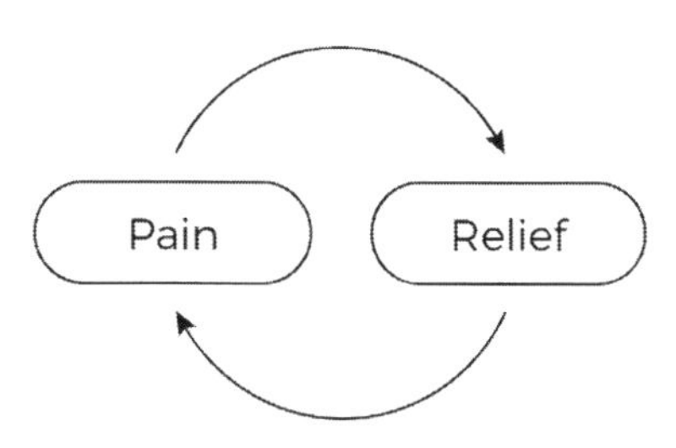

When I first read Gay Hendricks's book, *The Big Leap*, one line shook me to my core. He posed the question: "Am I willing to feel good and have my life go well *all the time*?"

My mind was blown. I had never entertained that as a possibility!

I decided to work on shifting my focus. I would ask myself, What's going well? What am I celebrating? What am I grateful for? What's right about this situation that I may not be seeing? I helped my clients shift their focus, too, with questions like: "What part of your body feels great? Would you be willing to expand that feeling?"

Slowly at first, then as I became even more skilled in shifting my focus, with increasing consistency, I started to experience more magic in my life. Everything just seemed easier. More opportunities came my way, or maybe I was just able to see them now. I felt lighter. My moods were less volatile. I felt like I stepped off the emotional roller coaster.

My clients were experiencing the same results too. Like Kevin, who was always worrying about money. He thought he was being responsible by focusing on his ever-growing mountain of debt and the bills he had to pay. He was, but it left him feeling stressed and anxious—even when he *did* have enough. It seemed his every waking moment was centered around his need to make more money. Kevin thought he was being resourceful by focusing on opportunities to make more money, and while that was also true, the energy driving his actions and feelings was coming from fear, scarcity, and lack.

Like energy attracts like energy. It's a law of physics. You can't come from scarcity and lack and get abundance. If your shirt is hanging in the bedroom closet, you won't find it by searching in the hall closet.

I gave Kevin a gratitude exercise to help him shift his focus from scarcity and lack to abundance. I also had Kevin make a list of how he thought having more money would make him feel. He used words like safe, free, happy, relaxed, and creative.

In doing this exercise, Kevin came to realize that his constant worry and non-stop hustling was actually not aligned with any of those feelings or the energy of having money. We then brainstormed some ways he could tap into those feelings—now—*before* he made any more money. We created some affirmations and he was consistent in visualizing the outcome he desired instead of scaring himself to death!

I'm happy to report that Kevin went on to double his income that year while feeling happier and having more fun! He also reported new opportunities "falling into his lap" seemingly "out of the blue."

Focus is where you are putting your attention and your energy. Perspective, on the other hand, is the lens through which you look at the object of your attention. It's how you are choosing to look at yourself, others, a situation, life, the world, and so on. It's the angle you look at something from. Perspective is everything, and the good news is, it can be changed!

It's important to look at your perspective because it will determine how hard or easy the next step of the process—Take Transformative Action—will be. I don't know about you, but I have a preference for ease and grace.

Where are you looking for guidance? As we discussed, most of us are conditioned to look outside ourselves, so we don't develop the skill of looking within to connect with our inner guidance and learn to trust it.

There are certain answers that can only be found within you, so building the skill of focusing *within yourself*—through body awareness, mindfulness, and meditation practices—strengthens your ability to hold your internal focus. This allows you to stay present in any given moment and maintain your external focus—which in turn impacts your productivity and your connection with others.

Here's a formula I like to use:

Focused Attention + Intention =
Increased Presence + Power + Connection

Now that you understand the power of focus, let's look at some practical ways you can improve this skill.

SLOW DOWN

When life wants to get our attention, it slows us down. We get sick. We get a severe case of vertigo. We get laid off from our job or a relationship ends and we suddenly find ourselves with a lot of free time. You get the picture. When we finally slow down, whether by force or choice, we gain a different perspective. We can focus on different things, or on the same things in a different way.

If you want to slow yourself down, here's a quick and easy way:

TRY THIS EXERCISE

Close your eyes. Shut out the world for thirty seconds and tune into your breath. Slow your breathing down to a count of six seconds per inhale and six seconds per exhale. Repeat three times, then gently open your eyes.

SIMPLIFY

When you have fewer things competing for your attention, it's easier to focus. That's why distraction is an effective way of splitting your focus. Our fear will always have us make things more complex and complicated as a way to stop us from moving forward.

Periodically take stock of where you are investing your time, energy, and money; and let go of what no longer feels aligned for you. This will allow you to give more focus to what really matters now.

Decluttering your space and letting go of everything that doesn't bring you joy, or that you don't use, will free up energy that you can direct somewhere else.

CREATE A MORNING RITUAL

I recommend having different practices and tools that help you to start your day by focusing internally—on how you feel and how you would prefer to feel. These practices can also help you establish an external focus for your day so that you know where you want to direct your energy and attention.

I've provided an example of a simple morning ritual on the next page.

TRY THIS EXERCISE

Before you get out of bed, or when you are in the shower, connect with each part of your body and acknowledge it with gratitude.

Gently stretch and move each part to awaken it. Consciously take three deep breaths, each time taking in more air. With each exhale, imagine releasing any stress or tension you may be holding onto.

Name five things you are grateful for.

Choose what you want to feel and receive that day. For example: "Today I choose peace, connection, joy, and energy."

KEEP A GRATITUDE AND SUCCESS JOURNAL

TRY THIS EXERCISE

Every day, write three to five things that went well that day and that you're grateful for.

Gratitude is a high-vibration energy. When you focus on the things you're grateful for, you will attract more opportunities and experiences that make you feel grateful. This also strengthens your self-esteem and self-confidence.

Which of these will you put into practice? Each one has the ability to have a profound impact on your life.

In the next chapter, we'll dive into the final step of this process—Take Transformative Action—because nothing changes without action!

CHAPTER 8

STEP 5: TAKE TRANSFORMATIVE ACTION

It's 8:00 p.m. on a Sunday evening in 2012 and I'm in the waiting room of the ER at the local hospital. The pain in my right lower abdomen and leg is excruciating. It's hard to sit still, but it's also painful to stand or walk. I am trapped between the need to move to relieve the pain and the fear of moving because it aggravates the pain in a different way.

The uncomfortable chairs and seeming indifference of the staff to my situation make the waiting even more intolerable. I just want something to stop the pain.

There is nothing harder than waiting when you are in severe physical pain. Waiting for help, for the pain medication to take effect, for them to figure out what's wrong–the feeling of powerlessness is maddening. The ensuing stress creates a level of emotional pain and tension that only exacerbates the physical pain.

Finally, around 5:00 a.m., I am given morphine. Sweet relief. But, despite the battery of blood tests, MRIs and CAT scans, the doctor has no explanation for my severe pain. He sends me home with pain medication and instructions to follow up with my primary care doctor. When I do, she diagnoses me with hypertension, puts me on medication, and refers me to my gynecologist, who then surmises the pain must have been caused by a degenerating fibroid.

Not getting definitive answers from the medical professionals, I turn within to seek the guidance of my soul—the aspect of me that has all wisdom, knowledge, and understanding, that knows every aspect of me.

I honored what I was feeling and began tapping on my frustration and the physical pain. I sought insight from my soul through prayer and meditation, taking long walks in the woods near my home, sitting quietly, focusing on my breath, placing my awareness in the area of my heart and listening. I had learned these practices during my yoga teacher training many years before.

Clarity came a few days later in the form of an internal "aha!"—an inner knowing. It was time to move on from my job at the hospital. My job was easy and comfortable, but my heart wasn't in it anymore. It was no longer bringing me the joy or fulfillment I desired and, ever since my near-death experience in China, my body, mind, and soul would no longer allow me to settle. It was time to put my energy into my small but steadily growing coaching business.

I had become a life coach three years before and was discovering a whole new way of working with clients. This allowed me to interact with the *whole* person and use all my skills. Even though my coaching practice was gaining popularity, I didn't yet trust my expertise in this new field, so I had been reluctant to let go of my part-time physical therapy job at the hospital.

In hindsight, I realize that this represented so much more than leaving a job. It represented switching from a career where I had achieved mastery and received recognition, respect, and great financial compensation. It meant letting go of something stable for something that was unsure.

Intense physical or emotional pain has always been my wake-up call, urging me to **P**ay **A**ttention **I**nside **N**ow. If I ignore it, it gets stronger, more insistent, prodding me to take notice and to take action when fear has completely immobilized me, or complacency has caused me to procrastinate for too long.

Just last weekend it happened again. A severe pain surfaced in my left hip. These days, I respond much quicker, from a place of curiosity versus judgment, and I quickly recognize its message. In this case, I was sitting too much while writing this book. I wasn't exercising and had forgone my massage and acupuncture appointments. I took immediate action to make the changes.

This pain was my body conspiring on my behalf to get me back on track with my self-care routine.

Pain is my ally. It knows I *hate* to feel it. I will take action, if the pain is strong enough.

You will too. That's how it serves.

This final step of the SHIFT process is about taking transformative action. The goal of your pain is to get you to change something, and nothing changes without action. It's important to note that the transformative action your pain is inviting you to take is intended to improve your life.

Pain can get you to stop or move. Both are actions. Both can be transformative. Sometimes you have to stop first and get clear so that when you do move, it is intentional, directed, and purposeful.

So how do you know what action the pain is trying to get you to take?

Next, you want to ensure that your actions are aligned with, and move you toward, the things you have identified in Step 3. These are the things you want to feel, to be, do, have, experience, and accomplish. Taking these aligned actions, consistently, is what makes them transformative.

Your beliefs are also an important consideration because they drive your behavior and your feelings. I developed the Quick SHIFT Process™ to enable audience members attending my talks to experience what I was describing. I wanted to share a valuable process that had helped both myself and my clients to get unstuck and into action—without bypassing or suppressing their emotions.

Too often, we get derailed by our emotional state, and it stops us from taking action toward our goals and desires, or we ignore our emotions completely and push through, which can derail our health and well-being. This process allows you to honor your feelings, identify the beliefs driving them, and focus on the ones that will lead to transformative action, so you keep moving forward in the most powerful way.

THE QUICK SHIFT PROCESS™

Bring to mind something you are struggling with, that you are stressing about, or that is causing you pain, then complete these sentences.

Write the first thing that comes to mind. Don't overthink it. When you get to the final question, write whatever action pops into your mind—even if it doesn't seem logical. You are accessing your innate wisdom through this process.

- Step 1: I feel ...
- Step 2: What am I believing that is making me feel this way?
- Step 3: I would prefer to feel ...
- Step 4: What do I need to believe instead to feel this way?
- Step 5: What is one action I can take that is aligned with this new belief?

(Continued on next page)

Here's an example of the Quick SHIFT Process at work::

- Step 1: I feel anxious, afraid, unsettled, scared, hesitant.
- Step 2: I believe that I don't have enough money coming in.
- Step 3: I would prefer to feel calm, confident, safe, free, happy, excited, trusting.
- Step 4: I choose to believe that money flows to me abundantly no matter where I am or what I am doing. I always have more than enough.
- Step 5: I will book the villa for my birthday trip.

Connecting to your inner wisdom will lead you to the action that ultimately relieves your pain. The key is to then act upon the insights and information you receive. The relationship you have with yourself—how connected you are with your body, mind, and soul, and the trust you have in these aspects of yourself—directly impacts your ability and willingness to take action.

This connection gives you clarity, and the trust gives you the courage and confidence to take action in the face of fear or seemingly insurmountable obstacles.

I have come to see that *this* is the root issue at the heart of most resistant emotional and physical pains: lack of connection to your authentic self and lack of trust in yourself. Any shame and judgment of that authentic self blocks that connection and creates or increases pain.

As I said previously, pain can get you to start taking action—but it can also stop you in your tracks.

Pain can stop you from taking action, thinking clearly, or moving forward. Sometimes, this is the most transformative action you can take. When you stop doing something that is creating more pain or that is not creating the results you want, it can change your life—just like when I needed to stop going to a job that no longer lit me up, so that I could make space for one that did. This was also the case when Teri had to stop giving services to a client that wasn't paying her. This allowed her to stop feeling resentful. We also see this when a severe pain from a sprained ankle stops us from being able to walk on it—preventing us from causing further injury.

And sometimes, the most transformative action you can take is to start doing something you haven't done before. This usually involves moving out of your comfort zone and doing something different, to get a different result. This was the case with my client George, who was struggling with depression. As we explored why he had lost his connection to his joy, I had him make a list of the things that brought him joy. In doing the exercise, George realized he had stopped doing the things that he got the most joy from. He made it a priority to do one thing from his list each day, and in time, his depression lifted.

When pain causes us to stop, we sometimes lose our momentum, inertia sets in, and it can be hard to get started again. Our fear of experiencing the pain again can also keep us from moving, and we get stuck. If this is what you are experiencing, there is no shame in getting help and support. Sometimes asking for help is the most transformative action you can take!

TRY THIS EXERCISE

Think about something you want to change, experience, or accomplish. (It may help to refer back to your work in Step 3.) Then ask yourself:

What do I need to stop doing to have this?

What do I need to start doing to have this?

See what answers organically pop into your mind and write them down.

The start/stop exercise leads us to another transformative action: letting go. You have to be willing to let go of where you have been to be fully present where you are now. And as we discussed earlier, your presence powerfully impacts your levels of awareness, connection, and choice.

You also have to be willing to let go of where you are now, so you can step into new and bigger possibilities. Are you willing to let go of the old hurt, or the stories that cause you pain? Are you committed to being free of pain? If so, what are you willing to do about it?

I love this quote by spiritual entrepreneur and teacher, John Assaraf: "If you're interested, you'll do what is convenient; if you're committed, you'll do whatever it takes!"

Inevitably, when we commit to making a change and start taking actions that move us out of our comfort zone and into the unknown, this activates some level of fear. It's a normal protective mechanism. We have to expect it, plan for it, and learn how to move through it. As you open to it with curiosity, you can learn to discern how it is here to serve you, like everything else that shows up in your life.

Here is a powerful affirmation for creating change: *I am willing to release the resistance. I am willing to change!*

Resistance is a symptom of fear. There are two things that stop us from taking transformative action—pain and fear. It is important to remember they are both here to serve you. Working with them, versus fighting against them, will help you move through them with ease and grace.

The only way out is through, but you get to choose how you move through. You can get to your destination by taking baby steps or a big, bold leap! Would you rather make your way into cold water slowly, allowing your body to gradually adapt? Or would you rather get it over with quickly by submerging yourself all at once? Neither way is right or wrong.

Working primarily with high achievers like myself, I know that too often we value pushing through the pain, and generally believe that the greater the effort we expend, the greater the value of the outcome. Not only is this a false assumption, I've experienced firsthand, and witnessed too many times, how much pain and suffering this perspective creates.

Transformative actions can be small, as long as they are consistent. That's what will create new neural pathways and new habits. The best way is through creating daily, weekly, or monthly rituals that build healthy habits

The consistency of your transformative action is fueled by the intensity of your desire and your level of commitment to making a change. Being clear about why you are making these changes—as well as writing it out and reviewing it regularly—will help you stay focused toward your goal. Having a strong *why* is the fuel that will keep you moving through the inevitable challenges that are part of any process that involves change. To stay motivated to meet your goal, your *why* has to be stronger than your fear.

For too long we have used pain as a motivator. We can unconsciously create pain to get ourselves moving, as I shared in many of the experiences in this book. I hope by now you have begun to see the advantage of changing your perception of, and your relationship with, pain. Now I invite you to do the same with fear. Love and fear are two sides of the same coin. The extent to which you are focused on one is the extent to which you are not focused on the other.

Love is the vibration and energy of healing. Love creates flow, expansion, and connection. Fear creates contraction, tension, and constriction, which slows down or disrupts the healing process. If we are going to heal our pain, we need to spend more time in a state of love, and to enable this, we have to change our relationship with fear.

Have you ever noticed that what you fear the most you seem to attract? So, as counterintuitive as it may seem, I invite you to acknowledge and feel your fear fully. What sensations does it create in your body? How intense is it?

Drop in fully and feel it, and see what happens. Remember, taking slow, deep breaths will help.

Fear is a natural part of life, so I invite you to embrace it. This is about the attitude you exhibit as you acknowledge it–being open, welcoming, inviting, curious, and loving. The antidote for fear is love, and love embraces. Welcoming the fear negates the need for resistance and allows you to feel it fully and see it through the eyes of truth. Most fear is **F**alse **E**vidence **A**ppearing **R**eal. Don't be afraid to question your fearful thoughts. Shine the light of truth on it by simply asking, "Is this true?"

Releasing judgment of the fear allows you to be in a state of acceptance. Acceptance is a subset of love. It in turn helps to release judgment, keeping things in flow so you don't get stuck. Accept the gift the fear is bringing you.

Consciously moving through your fear in these ways is taking transformative action.

Many times, we unconsciously hold on to the fear as a means of staying in the comfort of the known, no matter how painful or dysfunctional it might be. If this is true for you, start by accepting that this is where you are. Love yourself right there. Love is *always* the antidote to fear.

While fear is undoubtedly a powerful motivator, it's always more delightful and fun to move toward something you desire than to run away from something you fear. That's why in our coaching programs we are always helping our clients to focus their attention on their desires versus their obstacles. We start with acknowledging and exploring their pain because it helps to clarify what the desire is.

This was the case with my client Carmen, who, after a devastating emotional and financial loss, was left with her life savings of $250,000 decimated. Most shocking of all was the fact that she had always been a responsible person, saving diligently and investing wisely. As a result, this experience had not only wiped out her savings and sense of financial security, it demolished her self-confidence and eroded her joy. Carmen was riddled with anxiety, not sleeping well, and having panic attacks. She was in deep pain.

In one of our sessions, she expressed a desire to restore her financial cushion because of the sense of safety and security it gave her.

"What if this experience was an invitation to cultivate a sense of groundedness, safety, and security that was always there, whether you have money or not?" I asked. Carmen looked dubious. Her mind was not ready to contemplate that possibility, so I asked: "What amount of money would it take to make you feel safe and secure again, financially?"

"At least $100,000," she replied.

"When would you like to have that by?"

"Next August," Carmen said. It was currently mid-September.

I looked at her with a playful sparkle in my eye. "What if you could have $50,000 by the end of November *this* year?"

Carmen giggled with excitement and her face lit up. "That would be amazing!"

I immediately acknowledged that her mind had no idea how this would happen, and that that was okay! Her only job was to be committed to being in the energy of excited anticipation and joyful delight that she felt when she had imagined having $50,000 by the end of November.

Carmen took transformative action, focusing daily on doing the things that brought her joy. She also resumed her meditation practice, exercise, and self-care routine. She got creative and used her credit card points to buy a ticket home to spend her birthday with her family and best friends.

The end of November came and went. No $50,000.

When we spoke in early December, Carmen was still concerned about money but sleeping better at night. Her sister had given her some money for her birthday with explicit instructions to buy something nice for herself—not to use it to pay bills or lower her debt. "Coincidentally," Carmen had been contacted the day before our call by a jewelry store she had bought items from in the past, about a ring that was part of a set she had bought from them. It was the only one left and it was in her size. Did she want it?

Carmen wanted it! But the money her sister gave her wouldn't be enough; she would have to add a few hundred dollars to get it. Her fiscally responsible self was conflicted about doing that when she had so much debt.

I had Carmen check in with her body by asking herself, "Do I really want this ring?" Her body felt light and happy—that was her internal "yes!" Then, I had Carmen connect with her heart and ask, "If I buy this ring, will it make me money?" This is a tool I learned from Dr. Dain Heer.

Again, Carmen's whole body lit up with an undeniable "yes!" She took action immediately, sending an email to inform the jeweler she would take the ring.

A week later, Carmen sent me a text message that said: "The ring is already making me money!" When we spoke, she told me the day before she had gone online to ensure her pay had been deposited and found an extra $6,400 in her account! She had received an unexpected performance bonus from her job! We celebrated this "windfall."

Then, in mid-December Carmen got a cancer diagnosis. Because she had been focusing so diligently on feeling good, this news was perplexing and scary. It threw

Carmen back, temporarily, into the victim consciousness she had been living in previously, before we started working together.

I invited Carmen to consider the possibility that her cancer may have been created by the incredible stress that she had been under for the previous two years, and that it was not a representation of where she was now. I invited her to be curious as to how the cancer was here to serve her, and I reminded her that she got to choose how she moved through the experience.

Carmen chose to move through it powerfully, trusting that it was here to serve her in some way. She kept focusing on her joy, and the miracles kept coming. She was able to get a consultation with an oncologist in less than a week, right before Christmas. And when she called to reschedule her flight home, the new flight was $300 less!

The last week of December I got a call from Carmen. Her sister asked her whether she had any additional insurance policies that would help to cover her medical bills. She suddenly remembered that she did! And when she called her agent about it, she found out that it paid out $88,000 immediately in a lump sum upon diagnosis!

"And I'm not done!" Carmen continued. "I checked an old investment account I have and found it had tripled in value, and was now worth $24,000!"

When we added it all up, it was over $100,000! Carmen did not get the $50,000 by the end of November, but she had over $100,000 before the end of December.

Carmen is currently utilizing all the tools and perspectives she has learned through our work together to live through her cancer experience joyfully, powerfully, and intentionally. She chose an uplifting perspective on her situation and is making choices that are aligned with her authentic desires and intentions. Her medical team is amazed at her positive attitude, and she has a host of family, friends, and loved ones supporting her and cheering her on.

This is what's possible when you learn to embrace the SHIFT process. It doesn't matter where you start. It doesn't matter what the source of your pain is. You can choose new, more empowering perspectives and beliefs. You can open yourself up to accept the gifts your pain is inviting you to receive.

In our next section, we will look at how you can integrate this process into your daily life so you can have more joy, ease, and flow—no matter what life brings.

PART III

RECEIVING THE GIFTS OF PAIN

CHAPTER 9

INTEGRATING SHIFT INTO YOUR DAILY LIFE

Beep. Beep. Beep. The alarm goes off on my phone, breaking my intense focus on writing. I've been at it since 5:00 a.m., for nearly three hours. Time to move from my favorite writing spot—a comfy sofa in what my husband, Gary, and I call the "East Wing"—to get ready for a client call.

I see Gary working at the dining table and suddenly remember ... *Crap!* Last night I told him I would walk our dog, Sadie, since he had an early meeting at the office. I sheepishly admit that I forgot and ask if he could do it. He graciously says yes. A wave of relief washes over me as I rush upstairs to get dressed.

Passing my youngest son Jason's bedroom, a wave of guilt hits me as I remember the conversation we had last night.

"Mom, can you take me to the eye center tomorrow for my LASIK procedure?" he asked.

"You're still doing that? I thought you changed your mind?" "Yeah, I decided to go through with it."

"What time is the surgery?"

"It's at 3:00."

"I'm sorry, honey, the training I'm in doesn't finish till 5:30. Can you ask Dad?"

Ugh. I feel like a horrible mother. As I hurriedly get dressed and run down the stairs to my home office, I'm thinking about all the things I've been juggling this week and all the balls I've dropped. I was supposed to have submitted another chapter to my editor two days ago. I hear myself say aloud, "Girl, you are failing on *every* front!"

I hear the self-judgment and respond aloud with com-passion: "Sweet One, you have a lot on your plate right now. You consciously agreed to each one of these things because they *matter* to you. Jason will be alright. Gary has your back. The book will get done. Everything always has a way of working out. You are in the process of getting more help and support, and this is temporary."

I take a few minutes to tap on what I am feeling and put things into perspective so I can be fully present for my client call. *Even though I feel like I'm failing on so many levels right now, I deeply and completely love and accept myself ...*

I quickly go back up to Jason's room to give him a hug and ensure he has a ride. I'm reassured as I hear that he is feeling comfortable and excited about his procedure. By the time I log on for my client call, I'm calm and centered.

This is what it looks like to integrate the SHIFT process in your daily life. It's comprised of many mini shifts, so it might be helpful to break this example down.

Here's the first scenario, with Gary:

- **Step 1:** I become aware I have broken an agreement with Gary.
- **Step 2:** I acknowledge what I am feeling–guilt–and release the judgment.
- **Step 3:** I identify a solution: I ask him to walk the dog.
- **Step 4:** I focus on feeling appreciation for my husband and all the ways he supports me.
- **Step 5:** I take transformative action by renegotiating with him immediately.

And here's the second scenario, with Jason:

- **Step 1:** I become aware that I feel guilty that I am not taking my son to his eye surgery appointment.
- **Step 2:** I acknowledge the judgment I have about not being a "good mother."
- **Step 3:** I identify the lie in the judgment and the way it makes me feel: guilty, anxious, and ashamed.
- **Step 4:** I focus on how I would prefer to feel: calm, grounded, confident, and happy.

- **Step 5:** I take transformative action by speaking affirming and encouraging words to myself, checking in with my son to ensure he has a ride, and asking how he's feeling about his procedure.

I share this story to demonstrate that there is no "mountain top" you arrive at, due to your personal growth, where you no longer feel challenged by life. A full and engaging life will *always* have challenges. It's how you interpret and respond to these situations that determines whether they become painful or not–and whether that pain is temporary or becomes chronic.

Over time, integrating this process into your life makes you more flexible, adaptable, and patient with yourself and others. You begin to look at yourself, others, and life through different lenses. Your feathers don't ruffle as easily and you enjoy a greater sense of peace. You are more compassionate and understanding when you see yourself and others in a state of overwhelm and emotional turmoil.

As a result, you'll create less pain and, when there is pain, you'll move through it with greater ease and speed.

When you choose to adopt the perspective that every experience is an opportunity to learn, practice, or heal something, you respond differently. You relax into your experiences instead of fighting them, allowing you to flow through them faster and more easily as opposed to getting stuck or struggling through them.

You may not be able to control all of life's circumstances, but you do have control over how you *respond* to them. Think about how Carmen managed her cancer diagnosis in the previous chapter. How we respond, choose to look at, and be with our circumstances can completely change the outcome of the experience and how it serves us. It can determine whether an experience is painful or not.

My mentor, Jack Canfield, teaches an equation in his book *The Success Principles* that demonstrates why it is so powerful to be able to shift your perspective and your reaction/response.

E + R = O

E is events, R is responses, and O is the outcome.

You may not be able to change the events of your life; however, you can influence the outcome through how you respond.

The thing that really impacts your responses is your perspective and your belief system, so that's why shifting your perspective and changing your beliefs is so powerful.

Over time, your reactions become responses and you live in choice, no longer at the mercy of your past conditioning and experiences. No more doing things out of obligation or because you "should." ("Should" is always somebody else's idea!)

My client Jasmine used to be wracked with anxiety,

guilt, and shame. A mother of three young children, which included twins, Jasmine would spend hours driving alone, and she would often park in her car, listening to music and smoking marijuana to calm her anxiety and overwhelm, before putting on her "I've got this!" mask and heading back home.

Alone in her car was the only place she found space for herself, but any peace and calm she did find was quickly replaced by guilt, shame, and anxiety as she walked in the door to gleeful cries of "Mummeee!" and children latching on to her arms and legs. She saw herself as a "bad" mother. She felt like something was "wrong" with her. The inner critic in her head was having a field day driving her self-esteem and joy into the ground.

Jasmine's shame ran deep. "I have a beautiful life. A husband that loves me deeply, healthy children, loving family and friends, financial stability, a beautiful home. I *should* be happy!" But she wasn't. Her husband and family couldn't understand why, and that made her feel even more disconnected, alone, and misunderstood.

As we worked together, Jasmine came to recognize how cut off she was from her own heart, how self-abusive her relationship with herself was, and how much her self-judgment was fueling her depression and pain.

As Jasmine learned to release her *judgment* of her anxiety, it became easier to embrace it and be curious about what it had to show her. She paid attention to the people and circumstances that triggered feelings of anxiety within her. She used tapping to stay present with, and move through, the immense energy of emotions she had unknowingly held onto by numbing them with marijuana, alcohol, and more socially acceptable forms of distraction like "busy-ness." We worked together, using various techniques to release trapped emotions in the tissues of her body and clear underlying imbalances in her physical, energetic, and emotional bodies.

As Jasmine and I worked together over time, we formed a bond of trust and safety, giving her a point of reference for what it was like to be a safe space for herself. Jasmine generally left our sessions feeling less anxious, more light and free. As she began to accept herself, she became more confident and comfortable in her own skin. It was easier to be present with herself and other people. She was more connected to her heart, which opened like a beautiful flower, and all her relationships blossomed as a result.

The thing to realize is that you don't develop these abilities in the middle of a crisis. A crisis gives us the opportunity to practice applying them, and to see how well we have learned them.

This is what personal development is about: creating a safe, loving, and authentic relationship with yourself. You are building the inner strength, resourcefulness, and resilience that allows you to weather life's storms with grace. You are honing the ability to reach out and ask for support when you need it, learning to resolve conflicts quickly, and respond to the stresses of daily life differently.

As I have said previously, small shifts over time add up to *big* transformations. What I've witnessed repeatedly, and experienced myself, is that as we grow and develop, we are ascending what I call the Spiral of Transformation.

We continually cycle through phases of awareness, clarity, and action in the process of personal growth. You will come to see that every step of the SHIFT process brings a level of awareness, clarity, and action.

If you keep moving through the steps and the process, you will inevitably find that there are some core issues or themes in your life. For a long time, mine were not feeling good enough, not trusting myself, and not feeling safe.

To get an issue resolved, you must take different actions, create new experiences, and accomplish goals that take your life to a new level. Each new level brings new opportunities for growth and expansion which can show up as pain.

If you are willing to keep growing, you will continually cycle through new levels of awareness, clarity, and action. It can feel a bit like "Groundhog Day" because the same core issues you struggled with at the previous level repeatedly come up to be "handled" at the next level. Many people fall into the trap of thinking this means they haven't made any progress at all, and start to doubt whether they will *ever* completely resolve their painful issues. They can feel like they are stuck going round and round on a merry-go-round ride because the coil on the spiral is very close together, as illustrated in the diagram below.

This is where having a community or mentor to remind you how far you've come and to encourage you not to give up is vital.

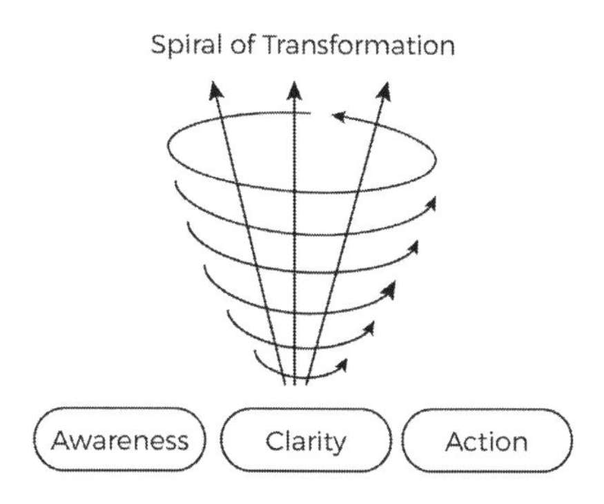

When you decide to take this journey of personal transformation, you will change, and your life will change. Not all of those changes will feel "good" right away—especially to other people. When you are no longer willing to give away your power, put your needs on the back burner, or silence yourself, some people may not like it. As you shift into this new, empowered you, you may need to part ways with some friends and family members who no longer support you. Old relationships may get put to the test as you emerge in a new way of being. Toxic relationships will end. You may feel lonely for a while until you make new, healthier connections and friendships.

The important thing is not to give up. These are part of the inevitable challenges of the journey. Having the support of a mentor and community makes this so much easier, and the changes are more likely to stick.

CONCLUSION

It's late on a Sunday afternoon back in 1993. The index finger on my left hand is numb from being pressed against the edge of the paint tray I've been holding for hours. I step off the ladder and observe my handiwork with pride. I've used a sponge painting technique on the walls of the treatment room in my office, and they now glow a warm reddish-orange in the ambient light from the lamp in the corner. It feels like a warm embrace.

Suddenly inspired, I climb back on the ladder to add one more touch. I use my right index finger to write in the still-wet paint:

Change Your Life. Change the World!

It is my hope for myself, my clients, and the world. It is something I have come to know is the truth as I have changed my own life and had the great honor and privilege to help others change theirs. I no longer live with constant anxiety. Most days I am so present in my body and my life that every choice is consciously made from a place of desire, love, and intention. It's how I continue to rise above hopelessness and despair despite having experienced and witnessed a world of pain.

If everyone changed their life for the better, the *world* would be changed for the better.

This is a difference I know we can make. I have seen how we humans impact one another. I know how hurt people tend to hurt other people, and that genuinely happy people infuse positivity into their environment and uplift others.

Imagine with me a world where people take 100 percent responsibility for their happiness and well-being, where everyone acknowledges their pain and makes self-love a priority. A world where everyone understands that it is possible to change their lives. A world where everyone is adept at shifting from fear to love, from pain to peace, and where this inner love and peace are reflected in the outer world.

Imagine being able to have a positive and profound impact on the entire world by changing just one life ... *yours*.

In the process of writing this book, I had new fears to face. On one of my daily walks, an exquisite blue butterfly joined me and stayed with me as if it wanted to share a message. I asked, and here is the message that came through:

Beloved.

Do not fear the dark.

It is in the depths of the places where the light does not reach that you must fearlessly go.

This is where shame hides.

We have to be willing to go into the darkness and shine the light there.

Hope transforms.

Hope gives life and brings light to the darkness.

Look for the opportunity that is being presented.

Ask what is desiring to be modified. Changed. Transformed.

When you realize that fear and pain are part of life, you can more easily accept it and look for the gift. This is where growth occurs. This is where freedom happens.

Are you ready to go into the fire? This is the fire that burns away illusions, that transforms, that releases, that sets you free.

This is living in your ultimate power and freedom.

Most people fear taking a risk because they are focused on what they may potentially lose versus what they stand to gain. What I know for sure is that while the process of transformation can feel very challenging at times, you stand to gain more than you could ever imagine: peace, love, abundance, ease, flow, acceptance, appreciation, connection, fulfillment, success.

This is the journey your pain is inviting you to take: to shift your perspective, reclaim your power, and transform your life for the better. It is not a journey your mind alone can take you on. You have to connect with and trust your heart, because it knows the way to your most amazing life.

RESOURCES

Learn more about Helen and SovereignMinds:

www.sovereignmindsllc.com

Connect with us on social media:

www.facebook.com/Sovereignmindsllc
www.instagram.com/oursovereignminds
www.linkedin.com/in/helenmacmillan/

Bonus gift: Experience the first week of our 12-week Journey Into Self-Love online program for free!

www.sovereignmindsllc.com/JiSL-free-week

ACKNOWLEDGMENTS

I have had many angels who have guided me, rescued me, encouraged me, challenged me, and loved me when I didn't love myself. They are too numerous to list them all, but I will mention a few here.

My mother, Ruth Stiebel, who is the embodiment of faith, tenacity, and strength. She was the first person to say, "You should write a book." Thank you for never giving up or running out on me, and for being an example of true grace.

My husband, Gary MacMillan. My rock. My greatest advocate. My best friend. Thank you for loving and accepting me unconditionally and teaching me how to do that for myself.

My children, Matthew and Jaime Gordon-Martin and Jason MacMillan. My greatest teachers and mirrors. Thank you for choosing me to be your mother.

My dear friends, Nicole Seaga, Gail Bell, Donna Peralto, Pam Niles, Monique Van Spankeren, Victoria Meeks, Andrea Rattray, and Penny Kerr. You have had my back in countless ways over the years. Thank you.

My cousin, Rosemarie Robotham-Arrindel. The most published and prolific author in the family. Thank you for being an example of commitment to your craft, for your encouragement to write this book, and for your magical editing abilities on the first shitty draft.

My mentors, Pragito Dove, Radavie Riom, John Milton, Anjel B. Hartwell, Jean Houston, Marcia Wieder, Monica Shah, Suzanne Evans, Larry Winget, Lisa Berkovitz, Kelly Epperson, Vanessa Shaw, Rich Litvin, and Darla LeDoux. You have stretched me, challenged me, enlightened me, held me to a higher standard, helped me to heal, motivated me to dream bigger, and forced me to acknowledge my beauty and brilliance. Thank you.

And finally, to my editor, Sally Mason-Swaab, and my publisher, Bryna Haynes—my "book doulas." You brilliantly held my hand, breathed with me, encouraged me, inspired me, and got this baby delivered into the world—finally! I am so deeply grateful for your expertise, your wisdom, and your love. Thank you.

This book has been a work in progress for over eight years. It has required me to acknowledge and move though many more layers of my own pain than I had previously, and to access the following gifts:

- Discover a new level of "wholeness."
- Deepen my understanding of, connection to, and love and appreciation for myself and my life.
- Uncover my truth, reclaim my power, and stand unapologetically in it.
- Unlearn a bunch of beliefs that no longer served the life experience I was desiring, and adopt new ones that are more aligned.
- Establish and hold strong, healthy boundaries.

I wish the same for you. Thank you, dear reader, for taking this journey with me.

ABOUT THE AUTHOR

Helen MacMillan is a master healer, life transformation coach, and wise woman.

Ever-evolving and answering the call to her next level of passion and purpose, Helen transitioned in 2012 from an illustrious thirty-year career in physical therapy and complementary wellness, to the life coaching industry. Her expertise in the area of creating joyful and sustainable success has featured in podcasts, television interviews, and print media articles, including the magazines *Essence* and *Ebony*.

Helen is the founder and CEO of SovereignMinds, a personal development and life coaching company that supports high-achieving, multicultural individuals in achieving the mental and emotional liberation that allows them to create success—without compromising their joy, health, and relationships.

A purpose-driven, heart-centered leader, Helen is committed to letting her soul lead the way. She considers healing her past emotional traumas, reclaiming her power, consciously creating a life of passion and purpose, and raising three amazing sons to be among her greatest accomplishments.

Born in Jamaica, Helen lives in the USA with her husband Gary and their dog Sadie. She delights in spending time in nature and FaceTiming with her granddaughter, Emilia.

ABOUT THE PUBLISHER

Founded in 2021 by Bryna Haynes, WorldChangers Media is a boutique publishing company focused on "Ideas for Impact."

We know that great books change lives, topple outdated paradigms, and build movements. Our commitment is to deliver superior-quality transformational nonfiction by, and for, the next generation of thought leaders.

Ready to write and publish your thought leadership book with us? Learn more at www.WorldChangers.Media.

WORLDCHANGERS
MEDIA

Made in the USA
Middletown, DE
06 September 2022